To Kill a Mockingbird

Harper Lee

Guide written and developed by
John Mahoney and Stewart Martin

Charles Letts & Co Ltd
London, Edinburgh & New York

First published 1987
by Charles Letts & Co Ltd
Diary House, Borough Road, London SE1 1DW

Illustration: Peter McClure

Stewart Martin is an Honours graduate of Lancaster University, where he read English
and Sociology. He has worked both in the UK and abroad as a writer, a teacher, and an
educational consultant. He is married with three children, and is currently deputy
headmaster at Ossett School in West Yorkshire.

John Mahoney has taught English for twenty years. He has been head of English
department in three schools and has wide experience of preparing students at all levels
for most examination boards. He has worked both in the UK and North America
producing educational books and computer software on English language and literature.
He is married with three children and lives in Worcestershire.

British Library Cataloguing in Publication Data
Mahoney, John
  To kill a mockingbird, Harper Lee.
  (Guides to literature)
  I. Lee, Harper – To kill a mockingbird
  I. Title II. Martin, Stewart
  III. Lee, Harper IV. Series 813'.54
  PS3562.E353T6

ISBN 0 85097 764 9

Printed and bound in Great Britain by
Charles Letts (Scotland) Ltd

Contents

Page

To the student   5

Harper Lee   7

Map of place-names   8

Understanding *To Kill a Mockingbird*   11
  (*An exploration of the major topics and themes in the novel.*)

Analysis chart   18
  (*This shows important events, where they happen, time sequence,
  characters, and where to find them in the text and this guide.*)

Finding your way around the commentary   21

Commentary   23

Characters in the novel   59

What happens in each chapter   65

Coursework and preparing for the examination   71

Studying the text   71

Writing the essay   72

Sitting the examination   74

Glossary of literary terms   77

To the student

This study companion to your English literature text acts as a guide to the novel or play being studied. It suggests ways in which you can explore content and context, and focuses your attention on those matters which will lead to an understanding, appreciative and sensitive response to the work of literature being studied.

Whilst covering all those aspects dealt with in the traditional-style study aid, more importantly, it is a flexible companion to study, enabling you to organize the patterns of study and priorities which reflect your particular needs at any given moment.

Whilst in many places descriptive, it is never prescriptive, always encouraging a sensitive personal response to a work of literature, rather than the shallow repetition of others' opinions. Such objectives have always been those of the good teacher, and have always assisted the student to gain high grades in 16+ examinations in English literature. These same factors are also relevant to students who are doing coursework in English literature for the purposes of continual assessment.

The major part of this guide is the 'Commentary' where you will find a detailed commentary and analysis of all the important things you should know and study for your examination. There is also a section giving practical help on how to study a set text, write the type of essay that will gain high marks, prepare coursework and a guide to sitting examinations.

Used sensibly, this guide will be invaluable in your studies and help ensure your success in the course.

Harper Lee

Nelle Harper Lee is an American, from Monroeville, Alabama, in the south of the United States. She was born on 28 April 1926, the youngest of three children. Her father was a lawyer. She was educated at Oxford, and also read law at State University, Alabama, but six months before graduating in 1950 she left to go to New York, with the hope of becoming a writer.

With encouragement and financial help from her friends she gave up the job she had taken during the 1950s in New York (with Eastern Airlines as a reservation clerk), and concentrated on full-time writing. In 1957 her first manuscript was submitted for publication, but she was urged to rewrite it. For the next two and a half years she worked on it and finally it was published as *To Kill a Mockingbird* in 1960, when she was 34. The book met with instant success and within two years it had won four literary awards including the Pulitzer Prize, and in 1962 was made into a film starring Gregory Peck. Since then Harper Lee has been a full-time writer, a contributor to *Vogue* and other journals.

Why was the book so popular? Its success was partly due to the topicality of the story. Negro civil rights was an issue that was slowly gaining support amongst whites in the 1960s. The appearance of the book coincided with this new awareness and Atticus's struggle to help Tom Robinson struck a chord with many readers. The simple narrative style, linked with its tongue-in-cheek humour, also contributed to its popularity, as did the dramatic and moving plot. The main characters, too, were well-drawn, realistic and appealing. Their dignity, strength and warmth were attractive to the reader.

The value of *To Kill a Mockingbird* extends beyond the local setting of a small Southern town in the 1930s. Its theme of having the courage to face up to difficult problems is universal. Its relevance is as strong now as it was 50 years ago.

Harper Lee returned to live in Monroeville where she spends her time writing stories and magazine articles.

SOUTHERN
STATES

*Atlantic
Ocean*

MISSOURI

VIRGINIA

TENNESSEE

NORTH
CAROLINA

SOUTH
CAROLINA

ARKANSAS

MISSISSIPPI

GEORGIA

TEXAS

LOUISIANA

FLORIDA

Gulf of Mexico

◄► ALABAMA ◄►

Seal of Alabama

The name "Alabama"
signifies "Here We Rest"
in the Creek language.

O ≈ *Fictitious places*

Peter McClure 1986

Natchez

MISSISSIPPI

LOUISIANA

Baton Rouge

New Orleans

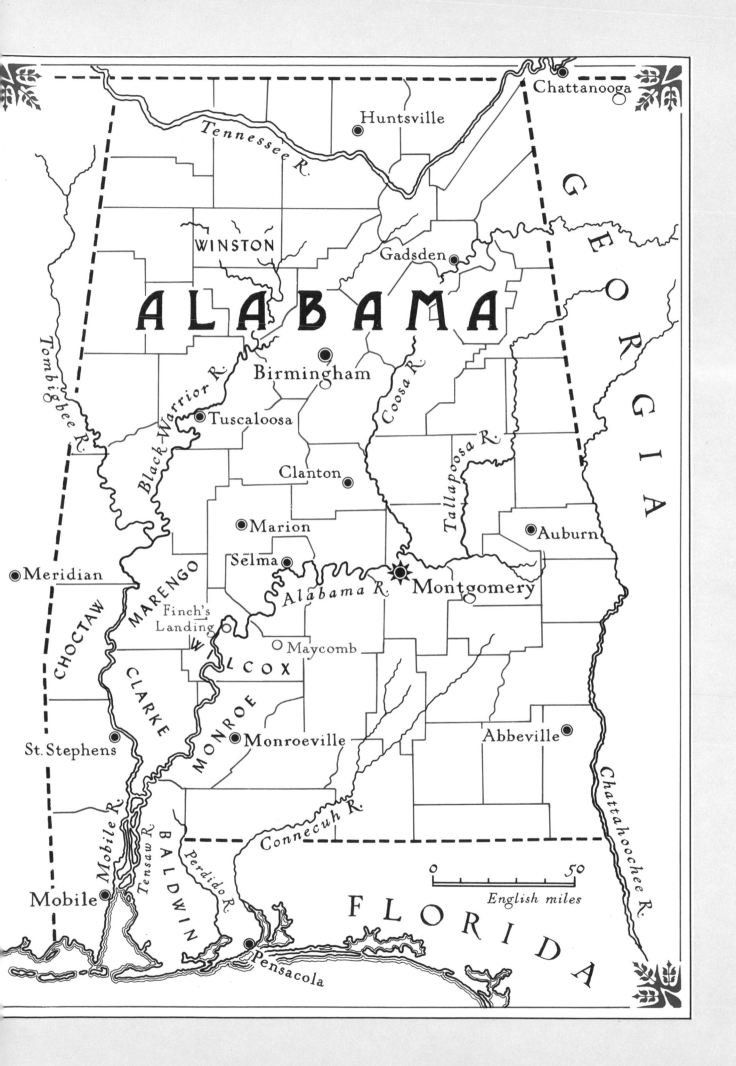

Understanding To Kill a Mockingbird

An exploration of the major topics and themes in the novel

Summaries of themes

Aspects of style

The device of an older person retelling incidents from their childhood is not uncommon in literature, and it is used in *To Kill a Mockingbird* to particularly good effect in two ways. Often Scout relates incidents that she does not fully understand, as happens in the case of Boo Radley, when Jem grasps long before she does that the items in the tree are presents from him to them. This technique allows the reader to think a little for himself, which adds depth to the narrative. Scout's incomprehension also adds a comic element. The second strength of looking at the story through a child's eyes is the impact it lends to the whole question of racial prejudice in the South. The injustice stands out because the children are aware of it for the first time.

However, because the story is written almost exclusively from a child's point of view, very little is stressed, emphasized or highlighted. Scout's style has a rather impersonal, flat and matter-of-fact feel to it which is out of keeping with her youthful, impulsive approach to life. Some of the scenes also suggest that they were written partly with a potential cinema adaptation in mind – and indeed the book eventually became an excellent film.

Humour plays a very large part in the book. Much of the novel deals with peaceful events in Maycomb, events which are often humorous. This forms a powerful contrast to the horror of Tom Robinson's trial, which is thereby emphasized. Humour relieves the tragic aspects of the story and adds a fresh and original touch to the narrative and it can be seen on many levels. The description of some of the characters' habits is amusing – Judge Taylor eating his cigar, Misses Tutti and Frutti, with their ear trumpet, cousin Finch reminiscing in chapter 9, and so on. The repartee between the children, and their innocent conjecture about the origins of babies is also very funny. Another large source of humour comes from Scout's ignorance of certain procedures, for instance at school when the teacher raps her over the hand, or her lack of knowledge about adult behaviour, and when she misunderstands Miss Maudie's retort to Miss Crawford about Boo Radley (where Miss Maudie wonders whether Miss Crawford invited her peeping-tom into bed with her!). Scout's innocence leads her to behave in unexpected and therefore funny ways. The most outstanding example of this is when she completely misreads the seriousness of the lynch-mob situation and starts up a friendly conversation with Mr Cunningham. The author uses satire when criticizing the education system and when she gently mocks characters like Aunt Alexandra, who is so sure she is always right, and Mrs Merriweather who is an amazing hypocrite. Atticus uses humour too, rather than anger, to point out to the children why their behaviour is wrong, or to take the tension out of an awkward situation, as when Dill is found under Scout's bed.

The overall structure of the book is well-crafted. Like many other good novels, incidents take place which make their full impact on us only in retrospect. Amongst other reasons, this is why such a novel always repays rereading and all students should therefore read any set text at least two or three times during the course of their studies.

Courage

We can recognize several kinds of courage in this book. There is the basic courage required to overcome childish fears, such as running past the Radley Place, or returning there to fetch the trousers that Jem caught on the fence. Atticus shows the same kind of courage in facing the mad dog, even though he has a gun in his hand. A more difficult form of courage to show is the moral courage that Scout has to find in order to face her friends without retaliating, when they call her father names. It cannot be easy to be made to look like a coward. The most difficult form of courage to possess is the courage to take on and carry through a task which is certain to end in failure. Atticus has to do this when he defends Tom Robinson. Mrs Dubose also chooses to do this, when she attempts to rid herself of drug addiction even though she knows she is dying and, in that sense, there is no point to her battle. She wins her fight, and Atticus calls her 'the bravest person' he knew. Atticus wants the children to realize that courage is not 'a man with a gun in his hand'. As an example of a man totally without courage we have Bob Ewell. Instead of facing Atticus alone Bob Ewell tries to take revenge on the children, and even then he does not have the character to face them in daylight, but strikes in the darkness.

Education

Education refers, in the strict sense, to the formal education the children get at school. The author is critical of this and makes fun of the way the educational system totally ignores the needs and abilities of the children. Miss Fisher is Scout's first grade teacher. She is new to Maycomb and is unfamiliar with the customs and habits of the people of the town. Some of the children give her a very hard time because of this. She shows an inflexible approach to education, clinging fixedly to her ideas and theories without regard to the realities of the classroom. Hence her struggles with Scout and her silly request that Scout must unlearn all she already knows about reading and writing and 'begin reading with a fresh mind'. In the next class the same lack of understanding of the children's background leads to failure. The current events lessons falter because the majority of children come from homes where the newspaper contains few 'current events'! On a more serious note the author criticizes the unconscious hypocrisy of the teacher who could condemn Hitler's persecution of the Jews and yet sees nothing wrong in the way the Negroes were treated in her own society.

Family and childhood

Because of the static nature of the Maycomb population, the same families had lived in the area for nearly two hundred years. As a result some people felt that each family seemed to inherit particular characteristics. They would say that a Cunningham could always be trusted or a Ewell was always dishonest. This led to great social divisions, when every family was categorized on a particular scale and it was most important to mix with the right family. Aunt Alexandra was particularly prone to this kind of snobbery. She tried to prevent the children playing with the Cunninghams, because of their lack of 'background'. Atticus was against this kind of social classification, preferring to judge a person on their merits as an individual.

The Cunninghams are a family of very poor farmers who live in Old Sarum in the north of the county. Their role in the book is varied and significant, but mainly they act as a contrast to the Ewell family. The Cunninghams are the honest poor. They never borrow what they cannot return. They pay their bills promptly, even if they have to pay in vegetables rather than money. They are quite independent of the State. The Cunningham's son, Walter, is poorly educated and has bad manners but Scout eventually recognizes (unlike her Aunt) that these things are not important. Walter is essentially a good child, whose circumstances have prevented him from learning to behave any differently from the way he does.

It is thanks to a Cunningham that the lynch mob disperses at the jail. Scout recognizes Mr Cunningham and by talking to him about private and family matters she makes him think like an individual again and not like a member of a mob. Finally, thanks to another member of the family the jury is delayed in returning their verdict. This delay gives both Atticus and Miss Maudie grounds for optimism for the future of their society.

Set in this context, the book presents us with an idealized form of childhood, where the narrator looks back to her own youth and selects important incidents and events. Thus we have an unusual and fresh view of the world through the innocent and often uncomprehending eyes of a child. All the virtues of children are there: we see their innocence, their frankness, their humour. We also see them starting to grow up; notice Scout's wry observation in chapter 13, that 'one must lie under certain circumstances and at all times when one can't do anything about them'. We notice the children's acceptance of people at face value, their lack of prejudice and pretence, their loyalty and strict obedience to childish codes. Their fresh outlook on people and events contrasts with the fixed, prejudiced ideas of the people of 'this tired, old town'. As Atticus remarks when the court verdict is greeted with no surprise by the majority of the townspeople, it 'seems that only children weep'.

The book opens with the quotation, 'Lawyers, I suppose, were children once'. The implication may be that children have an open, fresh approach to life and to other people which becomes muted in adulthood – especially so in lawyers, perhaps, because of their constant exposure to the way the legal system works. Is this interpretation true of the adults and children in the novel? Is it true in particular of Atticus? What other reasons might the author have had for putting this quotation at the start of the book?

The book traces the children's growing awareness of the nature of the adult world and the behaviour that is expected of them. For Jem the process begins naturally enough, with his disinclination to continue their childish games, and the adoption of an air of superiority towards his sister. The trial is a dramatic experience for him, however, and his total surprise at the verdict leaves him puzzled and at odds with the adult world. It takes him a long time to come to terms with the fact that people can allow such injustice. Scout, too, matures. She is fundamentally less self-centred than Jem and she learns to understand her Aunt and Boo Radley. She begins to shed her tomboy ways and realize the value of sometimes behaving with dignity, 'like a lady'.

Atticus is at odds with his sister about the way the children should be brought up. He has certain standards that the children have to follow but they are different from those of Aunt Alexandra. He expects the children to be respectful to adults, polite to guests, sympathetic to other people, and to try to use their reason rather than let their emotions get the better of them. He does not try to mould them to any set pattern of behaviour. He is tolerant of Scout's tomboy ways, her outgoing personality and her liveliness. Aunt Alexandra wants Scout to curb these characteristics, to behave like a lady, to be conscious of their social position as belonging to a 'good' family. After one attempt to make the children behave the way their Aunt wants them to, Atticus relents and allows them to behave as they have been used to.

History

History plays such an important role in shaping the people's attitudes that it is necessary to explain the background. The Civil War, which took place between 1861 and 1865, occurred when a group of Southern states, including Alabama, formed the Confederate States of America, and broke away from the main Union of States. After four years of bitter fighting they were defeated and rejoined the Union. One of the results of the Civil War was the emancipation of the slaves. Although in theory the Negroes were equal to the whites, in fact they continued to live separate lives, accepting their inferior status resignedly. In the 70 years since the war had finished, the situation when the story takes place (in the 1930s) had hardly changed. The Negroes were still segregated, and had only a glimmer of hope of any change. The novel is set at a time of economic depression which President Roosevelt with his 'New Deal' policy was trying to improve. The novel covers three years in the life of Maycomb county, during the Depression. The position of the Negroes in the Southern states had begun to change at the time Harper Lee wrote the book (in the late 1950s), with civil disturbances and rioting proof that the blacks no longer were prepared to accept their position as inferiors. The events in the book happen before the big Civil Rights movement, but after the Ku Klux Klan's activities had begun to wane.

Maycomb itself is a small town in Alabama. You can see its suggested locality on the map of Alabama which you will find on p 9. In the novel most of the population and that of the surrounding farming communities are poor. The population has remained virtually unchanged for decades, with the result that newcomers are not accepted easily. The ways of the people are set, and they have not been exposed to many twentieth-century inventions. Cars are few, cinemas nonexistent. The people are very religious, mainly Baptist or Methodist. Everyone knows everyone else, and local gossip is rife. Because life has progressed with so little change people's attitudes have changed little also. The Negroes are segregated and most people want them to remain so. Anyone who does not conform to accepted patterns of normal behaviour, like Mr Radley or Dolphus Raymond, is regarded as an oddity. So little happens that such major events as the rape trial are regarded as a day out for the whole county. It is a 'tired old town' that is long overdue for a fresh breeze of change.

Law

In theory all Negroes have had equal rights in law since the end of the Civil War in 1865. Yet, as is seen here, that does not always mean they receive justice. The author emphasizes this terrible wrong by making the reader look at the verdict through Jem's trusting, inexperienced eyes. Atticus still upholds his belief in the law for, apart from minor improvements which he agrees could be made for the better, he thinks it is satisfactory. What does need to change, however, are people's attitudes. The law can function, but justice cannot be dispensed until this change has come about. It is people who must apply the law to produce justice.

Judge Taylor is an honourable man who does his best to see that Tom Robinson has a fair trial by appointing Atticus to defend him. He is a good judge who keeps his court well-disciplined despite a rather casual air and some unusual habits, such as eating cigars and cleaning his nails whilst the court is in session. He is perceptive and sound for, as Atticus observes, his judgments are seldom reversed.

Mockingbird

The image of the mockingbird occurs frequently in the book. The children are warned that it is a sin to kill this songbird because all it does is sing. The mockingbird has no original song of its own, but merely copies the songs of other birds – hence its name. Both Tom Robinson and Boo Radley can be compared with this bird. They are both gentle people who have done no harm but only try to help others. Both their lives are a distorted version of what might have been 'normal' lives but for their individual circumstances and backgrounds, which neither of them has had the power to change. In different ways their lives are a mockery of the intolerant white society which surrounds them. Like the mockingbird itself Tom and Boo should be protected and cared for, not hunted down by the mob, who are full of false courage, ignorance and shallow pride like the children who shoot songbirds. Both Tom and Boo are persecuted, one by the jury and the other by the children and the gossips. The mockingbird symbol can also be applied to two important themes in the book: those of justice and childhood. Justice is 'killed' when the jury follow their own prejudices and ignore the true evidence. The innocence of childhood dies for Jem, Scout and Dill when they realize that the adult world is often a cruel and unjust place.

Prejudice

A dominant theme in the novel is the cruelty that people inflict upon others by the holding of preformed ideas, 'the simple hell people give other people', as Dolphus Raymond puts it. It is not just the matter of the deep racial prejudice which is present in Maycomb but the intolerant, narrow, rigid codes of behaviour that most townspeople wish to impose on others. This bigotry is made all the more menacing by being depicted as 'normal' behaviour by many characters in the book. Against the background of this small town such people as Boo Radley, Dolphus Raymond and, to some extent, Maudie Atkinson, are persecuted because they do not conform. Tom Robinson is found guilty, in the face of very strong suspicion that his accusers are lying, because he went against the accepted position of a Negro and dared to feel sorry for a white person.

So deeply entrenched and ingrained is the racial prejudice of the people of Maycomb that they do not realize the extent to which this leads them into hypocrisy. The author highlights such double standards during Aunt Alexandra's missionary circle tea. The women talk with great sympathy about the plight of the poor Mruna tribe in Africa, but later condemn the dissatisfaction of the Negroes in their own town. At school Miss Gates extols the virtue of American democracy where she says nobody is persecuted, unlike in Germany, and next is heard complaining that the Negroes are 'getting way above themselves'. Mr B. B. Underwood, editor of the *Maycomb Tribune*, is a similarly ambiguous character because whilst he despises blacks he also hates injustice. In contrast Atticus is the personification of honesty and straightforwardness. He is 'the same in his house as he is on the public streets', as Miss Maudie observes.

The Radleys are neighbours of the Finches and their house is an endless source of fear and fascination to the children. They hear frightening tales of what has happened to Arthur, the son, since he has been kept locked in the house. When Arthur Radley got into trouble at the age of 18 his father, a very strict Baptist, undertook to punish his son himself, rather than let the law do it. His punishment of his son seems very cruel. Since the incident 15 years before, Mr Radley has not mixed with his neighbours. On his death Calpurnia describes him as the 'meanest man God ever blew breath into'. His other son, Nathan, takes over the home and he seems no more friendly. It is he who shoots at Jem when he trespasses and he who blocks up the hole in the tree.

In contrast to the trial plot, the conclusion of which is no surprise to us, the Boo Radley plot is full of mystery and suspense. At first we do not know whether or not the eerie tales surrounding Boo Radley's circumstances are true. We are affected by the children's own fear and suspicions about the Radley Place. The mystery about the man remains to the end of the book, although we are gradually given clues which suggest that he is not the monster the children at first imagined.

Dolphus Raymond is also regarded as an oddity in the town, because he is a white man who chooses to live amongst the Negroes. He has a reputation as a drunkard but he tells the children that this is just a pretence. In fact he is a sensitive man who loathes the society which makes black and white people live separately. Interestingly the blacks in *To Kill a Mockingbird* do not seem to consider rebelling; the most that happens is that they become 'sulky'. They resent Tom's conviction but as they have been second-class citizens from birth they seem to expect it. Does this make the way they are treated 'right'? Why do you think people persecute others? Is it because they are full of hate, or because they feel threatened? Can you think of any modern examples of prejudice?

Religion

Most people in Maycomb are either Methodist or Baptist. Of the two, the Baptists are the stricter sect, the most extreme of whom interpret the Bible in a very narrow way which denies people any pleasure in life, even innocent pleasures such as growing flowers or going for a walk. Such rigid adherence to religious beliefs often causes people to act in an uncharitable, and arguably an un-Christian way. Mr Radley's treatment of his son certainly lacked compassion. The ladies of the Missionary circle were unkind to Scout while claiming to have the interests of poor Africans at heart. This narrow view of religion, with its emphasis on definite codes of behaviour rather than compassion for other people, adds to the intolerant atmosphere of Maycomb. In contrast to the attitudes of most of the whites, notice how the blacks are welcoming, as for example when Scout and Jem attend their church, the First Purchase.

Understanding

One of the main lessons Atticus teaches Jem and Scout is the importance of understanding another person's point of view. He urges them to stand in the other's shoes, to know how he or she is feeling. We see how successful Atticus is when the children learn to look with sympathy on Boo Radley, Mayella Ewell, and Mrs Dubose. Scout even learns to tolerate Jem's adolescent behaviour and reaches a better understanding of her Aunt. The book's plea for tolerance on racial matters is based on the idea that understanding is the key to greater equality amongst white and black people. The book is an unsentimental portrayal of enlightened views on the rights of blacks.

Violence

Behind the façade of this sleepy, hot, southern town, there is danger and potential violence. The deep hatred and fear that exists between white and black is a possible spark for violence. Look how the lynch mob, made up of normally reasonable, respectable men, are ready to kill and how they nearly succeed. Bob Ewell's hatred of Atticus nearly results in the death of Jem and Scout. Atticus's understanding of the danger perhaps explains his reluctance to boast about his skill with a gun. Although circumstances force him to use a gun, he does not want his children to admire his expertise. By pleading for tolerance and understanding instead, Atticus hopes to show the children how the causes of violence can be removed. Atticus is perhaps too idealistic here, because he wrongly judges the extent of Bob Ewell's hatred. In the same way, any hope that the racial problems of the South could be solved by tolerance and understanding alone was perhaps too idealistic. There were, for example, many race riots in the 1950s and 1960s in southern American towns, with much violence and killing.

Analysis chart

Analysis chart

'There are no clearly defined seasons in South Alabama; summer drifts into autumn, and autumn is sometimes never followed by winter, but turns to a days-old spring that melts into summer again.' – Scout.

Dates	1933			1934								
	Summer	September	September			Autumn	October	Winter	Christmas	February	Spring	Summer
Chapter	1	2	3	4	5	6	7	8	9	10	11	12
Important events	Dill arrives	Scout's first day at school	Burris Ewell attends school	Gifts begin to appear in the Radley tree	The children are caught with their note to Boo	Jem loses his pants in the Radley's yard	Nathan cements up the hole in the tree	Miss Maudie's house burns down	Uncle Jack arrives / Christmas at Finch's Landing	Atticus shoots the mad dog	Mrs Dubose dies	To church with Calpurnia
Themes Aspects of style	●	●	●	●	●		●	●	●			●
Courage									●		●	
Education		●		●								
Family and childhood	●	●	●	●	●				●		●	●
History	●	●			●	●		●	●			
Law	●		●									
Mockingbird										●		
Prejudice	●	●	●		●				●			●
Religion	●				●							
Understanding			●		●		●				●	
Violence												
Characters Atticus	●		●		●		●	●	●	●	●	
Aunt Alexandra									●			
Boo Radley	●			●			●	●				
Calpurnia	●		●	●								●
Dill	●			●	●							
Jem	●	●	●	●		●	●	●		●	●	●
Mayella Ewell												
Miss Crawford												
Miss Maudie					●			●				
Mr Ewell	●	●	●									
Mrs Dubose											●	
Scout		●	●	●	●	●	●	●	●	●	●	●
Tom Robinson												
Page in commentary on which chapter first appears	23	27	29	30	31	33	33	34	35	38	38	39

1935

Event	13	14	15	16	17	18	19	20	21	22	23	24	25	26	27	28	29	30	31
Month											End August, start September.			September	Mid-October	Hallowe'en			
Aunt Alexandra has arrived	13																		
Dill found under Scout's bed		14																	
Lynch mob arrives at the jail			15																
The trial begins				16															
Mr Tate and Mr Ewell testify					17														
Mayella Ewell testifies						18													
Tom Robinson testifies							19												
Dolphus Raymond talks to Dill and Scout								20											
The jury delivers its verdict									21										
Bob Ewell spits in Atticus's face										22									
Tom shot trying to escape from jail												24							
Tom's wife is told the news													25						
Miss Gates condemns Hitler														26					
Bob Ewell harasses Helen Robinson															27				
Bob Ewell tries to kill Jem and Scout																28			
Scout meets Boo Radley																	29		
It is agreed that Bob Ewell fell on his own knife																		30	
Scout walks Boo home																			31
Page	40	41	42	43	45	47	47	48	49	50	51	53	54	55	56	56	57	57	58

Finding your way around the commentary

Each page of the commentary gives the following information:

1 A quotation from the start of each paragraph on which a comment is made, or act/scene or line numbers plus a quotation, so that you can easily locate the right place in your text.

2 A series of comments, explaining, interpreting, and drawing your attention to important incidents, characters and aspects of the text.

3 For each comment, headings to indicate the important characters, themes, and ideas dealt with in the comment.

4 For each heading, a note of the comment numbers in this guide where the previous or next comment dealing with that heading occurred.

Thus you can use this commentary section in a number of ways.

1 Turn to that part of the commentary dealing with the chapter/act you are perhaps revising for a class discussion or essay. Read through the comments in sequence, referring all the time to the text, which you should have open before you. The comments will direct your attention to all the important things of which you should take note.

2 Take a single character or topic from the list on page 22. Note the comment number next to it. Turn to that comment in this guide, where you will find the first of a number of comments on your chosen topic. Study it, and the appropriate part of your text to which it will direct you. Note the comment number in this guide where the next comment for your topic occurs and turn to it when you are ready. Thus, you can follow one topic right through your text. If you have an essay to write on a particular character or theme just follow the path through this guide and you will soon find everything you need to know!

3 A number of relevant relationships between characters and topics are listed on page 22. To follow these relationships throughout your text, turn to the comment indicated. As the previous and next comments are printed at the side of each page in the commentary, it is a simple matter to flick through the pages to find the previous or next occurrence of the relationship in which you are interested.

For example, you want to examine in depth the aspects of style of the novel. Turning to the single topic list, you will find that 'Aspects of style' first occurs in comment 1. On turning to comment 1 you will discover a zero (0) in the place of the previous reference (because this is the first time that it has occurred) and the number 24 for the next reference. You now turn to comment 24 and find that the previous comment number is 1 (from where you have just been looking) and that the next reference is to comment 25, and so on throughout the text.

You also wish to trace the relationship between Jem and Scout throughout the novel. From the relationships list, you are directed to comment 21. This is the first time that both Jem and Scout are discussed together and you will now discover that two different comment numbers are given for the subject under examination – numbers 32 and 24. This is because each character is traced separately as well as together and you will have to continue tracing them separately until you finally come to comment 32 – the next occasion on which both Jem and Scout are discussed.

Comment number

Quote from novel

Previous appearance in guide

Character or idea under discussion

12   The misery of that house . . .
The Radleys are regarded as strange and different because they do not conform to the rigid patterns of behaviour that the Maycomb people expect. How much is this a fault in the Radleys? How much is it a fault in the people of Maycomb?

11/13   History
11/13   Prejudice

Next appearance in guide

Commentary

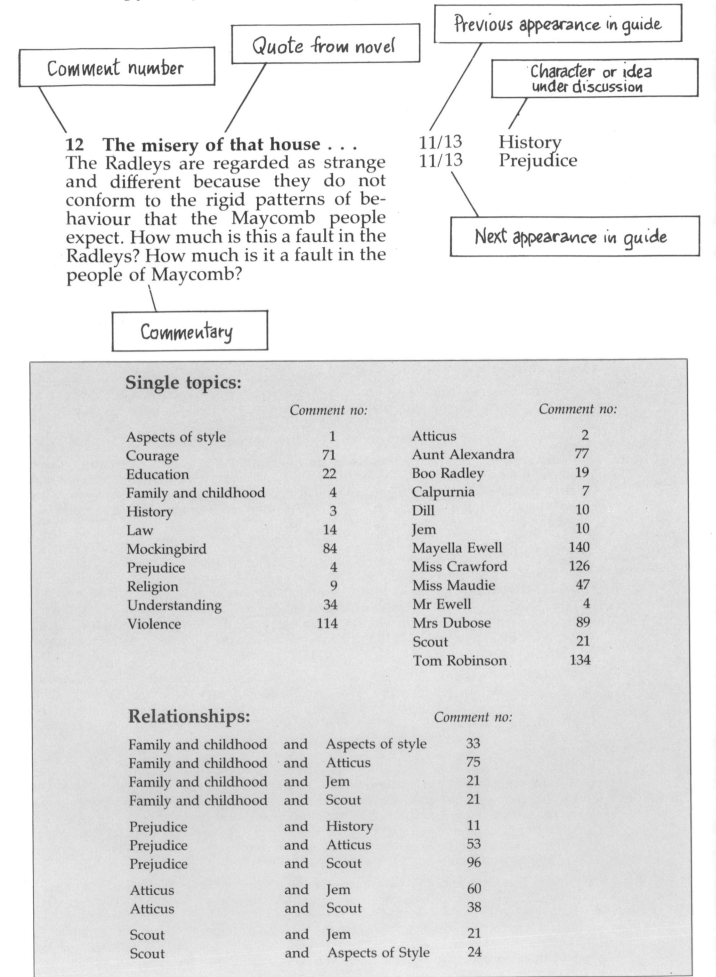

Single topics:

	Comment no:		Comment no:
Aspects of style	1	Atticus	2
Courage	71	Aunt Alexandra	77
Education	22	Boo Radley	19
Family and childhood	4	Calpurnia	7
History	3	Dill	10
Law	14	Jem	10
Mockingbird	84	Mayella Ewell	140
Prejudice	4	Miss Crawford	126
Religion	9	Miss Maudie	47
Understanding	34	Mr Ewell	4
Violence	114	Mrs Dubose	89
		Scout	21
		Tom Robinson	134

Relationships:

			Comment no:
Family and childhood	and	Aspects of style	33
Family and childhood	and	Atticus	75
Family and childhood	and	Jem	21
Family and childhood	and	Scout	21
Prejudice	and	History	11
Prejudice	and	Atticus	53
Prejudice	and	Scout	96
Atticus	and	Jem	60
Atticus	and	Scout	38
Scout	and	Jem	21
Scout	and	Aspects of Style	24

Commentary

Chapter 1

1 When he was nearly thirteen . . .
Look how much we learn in the first three paragraphs. We know the narrator's age at the time of the incident, the identity of Jem and Atticus, the names of most of the key characters, and the history of the Finch family who arrived in Alabama in about 1813. We also learn that the story is being related some years later. The narrator's age at the time of the incident is important, because it allows the novel to take advantage of two different viewpoints which are widely separated in time, to give a more complete picture of events.

If you have not already done so, read the discussion on 'Aspects of style' on p 11 of this guide. In some works of literature authors' personalities are not very prominent and it is hard to find out much about them, or their attitudes, from reading their work. We never seem to 'get to know' such authors as individuals.

In this novel we can see that there is quite a strong sense of autobiography in the writing. In the section entitled 'Understanding To Kill a Mockingbird' you can find out how this has influenced the general style of the novel, and how it has affected the way the reader is able to see the events which are described.

2 I said if he wanted . . .
The children's father was named after a Roman who lived from 109–32 BC. The Roman escaped to Greece during the Roman civil war and became such an important figure there that he was named Atticus ('Attica' means Greece). He refused to join with either side in the Roman war. Why is this an apt name for the children's father? Look at chapter 16 to get an idea of why this might be.

Read this part of chapter 1 carefully. Look at the map of Alabama and work out where you think Finch's Landing and Maycomb could be. Compare it with the places indicated on the map to see whether you agree with the places marked.

3 Simon would have regarded . . .
The 'disturbance' referred to is the Civil War, which was fought between the Northern and Southern states of America. Alabama, being part of the Southern Confederation, was on the losing side. Why would Simon Finch have been so annoyed about the 'disturbance'? For a clue, look at the paragraph on the first page of the novel which begins 'Being Southerners . . .'.

4 During his first five . . .
The importance of heredity and 'background' is a theme which runs throughout the book. We know that the Finch family have lived in this area for over 100 years. So strong is the family network that different families have become recognizable by definite characteristics. This explains the comment on the previous page that the Haverfords are all jackasses,

---

Characters and ideas
previous/next comment

0/24   Aspects
        of style

0/15   Atticus

0/5   History

0/27   Mr Ewell
0/8   Family and
        childhood
0/11   Prejudice

meaning that they are all fools. The Cunningham and Ewell families also seem to have been given particular identities. How accurate do you think these thumb-nail sketches are? How accurately does Aunt Alexandra see other people; the Ewells for example? To what extent does this tendency to 'pigeon-hole' other people contribute to the intolerance displayed by some characters in the novel?

5 Maycomb was an old town . . .
To understand the behaviour of the people of this small southern town we need to feel the atmosphere of the place. Look at what we are told about Maycomb. It is an old town, and therefore the same families have lived there for generations. It is a tired town, therefore the pattern of life has not changed for a long time and there is no desire for change. It is hot, therefore life proceeds at a slow pace. It wears people down just to live there. It is poor, therefore there is no money to change or improve things. Most importantly it is a town turned in on itself with no concern for the outside world, no real awareness of its existence and not much interest in finding out.

3/6   History

What does all this tell you of the likely attitudes of its inhabitants? As a rule would you expect them to be narrow- or broad-minded? The rest of chapter 1 contains some useful material which you could use to help you make up your mind. People's attitude towards education is revealing in this context. Notice how the children at the school have already acquired the values of their parents, and how it is this which causes their new teacher so many problems. This should not surprise you, because the way the children live and are being brought up is bound to influence their view of the world. This is something which is true of all of us. For example, do people who are intolerant and prejudiced usually come from backgrounds where the adults are prejudiced also? This certainly seems to be the case in the novel. How much influence on your own attitudes has your home-life had?

6 People moved slowly then.
The incidents in the book take place in the mid-1930s. This was a time of great economic depression in America, especially in the South. The only hope that things might improve came in the person of Franklin D Roosevelt, who was elected President in 1932 and offered the people a 'New Deal' and told them there was 'nothing to fear but themselves'. How true is this of Maycomb? To what extent is it the theme of the novel that people have only themselves to fear? Is fear the basis of all prejudice and intolerance? Look at the lynch-mob scene in chapter 15 as an example.

5/9   History

7 Calpurnia was something . . .
Although only the cook, her role in the family is obviously more important. Whose place did she almost take? (Read the start of the character summary of Atticus on p 59.) What was Atticus's attitude to Calpurnia? Consider what happens in chapter 14, when Aunt Alexandra wants to get rid of her. Judging from the narrator's comments that Calpurnia's hands were 'wide as a bed slat . . .' and that she was 'tyrannical', what do you think she was like with the children? How did the children regard her? Compare their attitude to her with their attitude to other ladies in the novel – Aunt Alexandra, for example.

0/18   Calpurnia

8 'I'm Charles Baker Harris,' . . .

Look at the direct way in which the children speak to each other. Imagine a similar conversation where three adults meet for the first time: how do you suppose it might differ from this conversation? What particular qualities in the way children behave is the author conveying here? Look at what they say to each other about the subject of reading. Interestingly, it is this same matter of reading which causes such a fuss with Scout's teacher, Miss Caroline Fisher, in chapter 2.

4/16   Family and childhood

9 Dill was from Meridian, . . .

What does Jem's remark 'don't have any picture shows here' reveal about the backwardness of the town? The importance of religion in the lives of the people of Maycomb is a significant factor in the book, and it is interesting that Jem should point out that the only picture shows they ever get in Maycomb are 'Jesus ones'. Is there any relationship between people's attitude towards religion and their attitude towards prejudice? Would it be fair to say that the most devoutly religious people tend also to be the most intolerant?

6/11   History
0/14   Religion

10 Dill had seen *Dracula* . . .

Why was Jem beginning to be interested in Dill? In what ways was Dill different from Jem and his sister? Look at the next page to see the contribution he added to their activities.

0/20   Dill
0/20   Jem

11 Inside the house lived a . . .

The mystery of the Radley Place was not sensed merely by the children. It became, for adults too, the object of superstition and fear. The author is building up a picture of the townspeople of Maycomb as people who are more influenced by feeling and narrow-minded doctrines than by reason.

Later on in the novel, in chapter 24, we hear about the African tribe of the Mrunas. Some characters regard the Mrunas as tribal savages, but is this description in fact better suited to some of the inhabitants of Maycomb? How tolerant and caring are the Mrunas? How tolerant and caring is Maycomb? Does Harper Lee seem to you to want to draw certain conclusions here?

9/12   History
4/12   Prejudice

12 The misery of that house . . .

The Radleys are regarded as strange and different because they do not conform to the rigid patterns of behaviour that the Maycomb people expect. How much is this a fault in the Radleys? How much is it a fault in the people of Maycomb?

11/13   History
11/13   Prejudice

13 According to neighbourhood legend, . . .

The Cunninghams are a family with a wild reputation who come from the surrounding countryside. Notice the close sense of community in Maycomb where people think they have the right, even the duty, to make the Cunninghams improve their ways.

12/15   History
12/14   Prejudice

14 The other boys . . .
What do you think of Mr Radley's behaviour towards his son? Is it in keeping with our previous knowledge of the family that he should decide to deal with the trouble himself? We learn on the next page that Mr Radley was a very religious man, who 'took the word of God as his only law'. Can you understand how he can behave so cruelly to his son and yet profess to be very religious?

0/37	Law
13/17	Prejudice
9/48	Religion

15 But there came a day, . . .
How does Atticus differ from most of the rest of the people of Maycomb? Contrast Atticus's reaction to that of Calpurnia. On a more general point, what is Atticus prepared to do that the people of Maycomb will not? (Read what Miss Maudie says about Atticus in chapter 22.)

| 2/36 | Atticus |
| 13/22 | History |

16 Nobody knew what form . . .
The innocence of childhood is apparent in Jem's thoughts that Boo Radley must be chained to the bed to make him stay in all those years. Atticus's experience of life and people tells him that there are 'other ways of making people into ghosts'. What sort of pressure might Boo's father and brother have exerted on him to make him stay inside?

The use of the word 'ghost' is very significant. Ghosts are things which are believed in only by superstitious people. Such people believe that ghosts come back to haunt places. The children talk about Boo Radley as being a 'haint' (ghost), but why do they do this? Is it only because he hasn't been seen for so long, or is there some other reason also?

Is there anybody, or anything, else in the novel that is made into a 'ghost' by the people of Maycomb?

| 8/19 | Family and childhood |

17 'There goes the meanest . . .'
The cruelty of Mr Radley towards his son is underlined by Calpurnia's comment. Why is her condemnation of Mr Radley particularly significant? (Look at why the children felt so surprised by her comment.)

| 14/18 | Prejudice |

18 'There goes the meanest . . .'
This is the first comment on the relationship between Negroes and whites. What do we immediately learn of the position of the Negro? Why should it be that Calpurnia so rarely comments on the ways of *white* people? (Think about the reason for Mr Gilmer's reaction, in chapter 19, to Tom's pity for Mayella Ewell.)

| 7/34 | Calpurnia |
| 17/27 | Prejudice |

19 Jem gave a reasonable description . . .
Look at Jem's description of Boo. Notice how it is a wonderful combination of imagination and reason. Children are credulous and will believe stories as long as they seem to agree with what they already think and as long as they seem plausible. How true is this also of some of the grown-ups in the novel? Think about the reactions of people at the trial of Tom Robinson.

| 0/40 | Boo Radley |
| 16/21 | Family and childhood |

20 Jem thought about it . . .
Notice the rivalry between the two boys? What does Dill say that finally makes Jem put 'honour' before 'his head'?

| 10/43 | Dill |
| 10/21 | Jem |

Chapter 2

21 Jem condescended to take me . . .
One of the most pleasing aspects of the book is the relationship between Jem and Scout. They are very close but according to Jem, once they are at school their friendship must stay private. Like all children, Jem feels he must conform in public to the behaviour of his friends. There is no room for his sister, a girl four years his junior.

This pressure to conform can also be seen in the behaviour of the adults in the book. Only individuals with strong consciences, like Miss Maudie and Atticus, can free themselves from these bonds. Comparing the attitudes and behaviour of the children at school with those of the adults in the 'real' world produces some fascinating parallels.

20/32	Jem
0/24	Scout
19/22	Family and childhood

22 Miss Caroline printed her name . . .
Look at the strong influence of past events on people's attitudes. Miss Fisher is regarded with suspicion because of her origins; she comes from a part of Alabama that stayed loyal to the North during the Civil War. People's memories are long – by the time of the novel the Civil War had been over for 70 years! North Alabama is seen as somewhere quite different from Maycomb because it is industrial, Republican and most significantly because the people have no 'background'. In other words, the people were relatively new to the area; they had not lived there for generations.

0/23	Education
21/26	Family and childhood
15/23	History

23 Miss Caroline began the day . . .
Miss Fisher's 'foreignness' is emphasized by her choice of story. She does not appreciate that the majority of her children come from a background that makes them 'immune to imaginative literature'. The use of the word 'immune' is clever, because it shows us how the people of Maycomb regard such things as imaginative literature. They regard it as so foreign, so threatening to their way of life, as to be comparable with a disease.

22/24	Education
22/29	History

24 I suppose she chose me . . .
The author is poking fun at the public education system here, where a teacher scolds a child for having already learnt to do what it is her job to teach her. Miss Fisher behaves absurdly by telling Scout to stop her father teaching her any more, because it will interfere with her reading. Scout's sense of fairness is outraged because she does not understand what wrong she has done, especially as no one has really ever taught her to read. Harper Lee is pointing out how far from the real world is the understanding of some of the children's teachers. Interestingly, it is these same kinds of people who are so quick to pass judgment on others later in the book.

21/25	Scout
1/25	Aspects of style
23/25	Education

25 'Don't worry, Scout,' . . .
The author gently mocks the teacher's faith in this new method of teaching reading. (Jem is mistaken about its purpose. The Dewey Decimal system is a popular method of classifying library books.) The rigidity of the school system is also criticized when Scout is told she must print, not write, for the next two years. In all Scout is not impressed with her first day at school. Are you?

24/30	Scout
24/28	Aspects of style
24/31	Education

26 I rose graciously . . .
Why does Scout think that the mention of Walter's surname will make everything clear? Does Scout perhaps assume that everybody else in the world is like the people of Maycomb? Is this a normal attitude in children? Is it the same attitude which many of the grown-ups in Maycomb also have? Remember what has already been said about family characteristics, and read 'Family and childhood' on p 12 for further information.

22/33 Family and childhood

27 My special knowledge . . .
The Cunninghams are proud, honest, poor but very independent. They will not accept charity from the church or government. They are the respectable poor, in contrast to the Ewell family who gladly receive help from the state.

5/35 Mr Ewell
18/29 Prejudice

28 My special knowledge . . .
Another form of humour in the book stems from Scout's innocent enquiries and statements. Here Jem is able to tease her about the meaning of entailment. (It is in fact a legal term to describe the settling of land on people other than the original owner so that no one person can then be the absolute owner of that land any more.) She obviously remembers the term because it plays an important part in a future situation (see chapter 15).

25/30 Aspects of style

29 Atticus said professional . . .
We gain an insight into the plight of the poor farmers in the South during the 1930s. Poverty forced them to mortgage their property or sign entailments (the previous comment explains what this means). This meant they needed hard cash to repay their debt. The government offered work in the form of welfare schemes that paid money, but taking the work would mean leaving their farms. People such as the Cunninghams, who were a 'set breed of men', were reluctant to leave their farms for such work because it would mean seeing their property go to ruin.

23/48 History
27/35 Prejudice

30 Miss Caroline stood stock . . .
This is another example of humour arising from Scout's innocence and ignorance. She is unaware of school practice and makes an incorrect assumption about why she has to put out her hand.

What do you think of Scout's behaviour on this, her first morning at school? Has she been outspoken and rude, or is she just unaware of the behaviour expected of her? Whose real fault is it that she is punished? Is this the sort of thing, on a more serious level, that happened to Boo Radley when he was young? Whose real fault is it that Boo has ended up the way he has?

25/32 Scout
28/33 Aspects of style

31 When Miss Caroline threatened . . .
Do you have any sympathy for Miss Caroline? Why has her task at school been so difficult this morning? Is it simply that she is new to the school? To what extent do you think her problems are caused by her not being from Maycomb, but from Winston County, in North Alabama? What advantage does Miss Blount, a native Maycombian, have over her? How tolerant is Miss Caroline of the children of Maycomb? How tolerant is Maycomb of Miss Caroline? (Notice how Miss Blount speaks to Miss Caroline.)

25/39 Education

Chapter 3

32 Catching Walter Cunningham . . .
The difference in temperament between brother and sister is quite marked.
Scout is hot-headed, and needs to settle an argument quickly by the only
method she knows–her fists. Jem is more reasonable. Look out for
similarities between Jem and his father. Atticus is a widower, and so we
cannot easily look out for similarities between Scout and her mother. Unlike
Jem, Scout does not remember her mother clearly. So who do you think
Scout becomes more like as she grows up?

33 Jem seemed to have little . . .
The repartee between Jem and Scout is often very amusing. With the normal
childlike desire for fairness and honesty, neither will let the other get away
with boasting, invention or lies. Look at how Scout deflates Jem's claims
about his behaviour in front of the Radley Place.

34 While Walter piled food . . .
One of the greatest lessons that Atticus and Calpurnia try to teach the
children is tolerance of other people's behaviour. That is why Scout is so
soundly scolded here.

35 The boy stood up.
Notice the difference in dress between Burris Ewell and Walter Cunningham. Burris's clothes were filthy; Walter's at least were clean if patched.
Look on the next page at the description of Burris's father. He is 'right
contentious' (argumentative). Of what is this a forewarning? (See what
happens in chapters 23 and 28.)

36 Atticus sat down . . .
The need to look at circumstances from the other person's point of view is a
strong theme in the book. It is the chief lesson Atticus tries to teach his
children. Notice on the next page how he tries to make Scout see the day at
school from Miss Caroline's point of view.

37 'Let us leave it at this,' . . .
Notice again how the Ewells fit into this pattern of family characteristics. On
the previous page Atticus points out that for three generations, they have
been 'the disgrace of Maycomb'. Notice how the law is bent slightly out of
compassion for the Ewell children. Why is this more possible in a small town
than it might be in a big city? Think about how everyone knows everyone
else's business in a small town, and how this can lead not only to the kind of
arrogance we have seen, but also to humanity and compassion. Look for
example at what Reverend Sykes says to his congregation about Helen
Robinson in chapter 12. How true is it that to know someone is to
understand them, as Atticus seems to believe? The Bible suggests that to
understand is to forgive, and whilst we might be able to forgive Mayella
Ewell, can we forgive her father? At the end of the novel can Atticus forgive
him, do you think?

Characters and ideas
previous/next comment

21/33	Jem
30/33	Scout
32/42	Jem
32/34	Scout
30/38	Aspects of style
26/37	Family and childhood
18/41	Calpurnia
33/38	Scout
0/36	Understanding
27/37	Mr Ewell
29/48	Prejudice
15/38	Atticus
34/55	Understanding
35/134	Mr Ewell
33/44	Family and childhood
14/122	Law

38 When Atticus looked down at me . . .
Notice how Atticus solves Scout's problem with reason and wisdom. Notice also his dry and subtle wit in stopping his impetuous daughter from clinching the agreement in the traditional Maycomb fashion!

36/53	Atticus
34/39	Scout
33/39	Aspects of style

Chapter 4

39 The remainder of my schooldays . . .
It is very much Scout the older person who is talking now. No child of six, however much she felt the boredom of school, could express her feelings in such a way. Knowing what you do of Scout and Jem's background, why would formal education be of so little use to her? See how she observes that 'Atticus and my uncle, who went to school at home, knew everything'. Is the author mocking the school-learning which Maycomb county is giving Scout?

38/41	Scout
38/42	Aspects of style
31/199	Education

40 Two live oaks stood . . .
The suspense about the Radley Place has been kept alive by constant references to Scout and Jem running past the door as fast as possible. A new development now comes with the appearance of chewing gum in the tree outside.

19/42	Boo Radley

41 Rather than risk a tangle . . .
Scout has always been resentful of Calpurnia's authority and we can see this in chapter 3, where Scout thinks that 'she had always been hard on me' – although the narrator (the older Scout) expresses this in a very tongue-in-cheek way! How far do you think the change in their relationship is due to Scout growing up and becoming more reasonable and how much is it because Calpurnia changes her attitude towards her?

34/94	Calpurnia
39/42	Scout

42 Finders were keepers . . .
What are we supposed to assume that Jem is thinking about? Has he connected these Indian-heads (one cent coins) with Boo Radley? Here is an interesting gap between Scout the narrator, who knows everything, and Scout the seven-year-old, who has not yet made sense of the situation. Notice how Scout observes that 'Before Jem went to his room, he looked for a long time at the Radley Place'.

40/59	Boo Radley
33/57	Jem
41/46	Scout
39/45	Aspects of style

43 Two days later Dill . . .
Dill enjoys the superior position that travel and life in a bigger town give him. He boasts, too, on the next page, of his father's position. However, Jem and Scout are not taken in by him. Why does Dill make up so many tales about his parents, his travels and his life in general? Is Dill essentially a lonely child? Is this why he says, at the end of Tom Robinson's trial, that he wants to become a clown?

20/54	Dill

44 One day we were so . . .
Do you think it likely that Atticus did know what the children were playing? It is a common mistake of children to assume that if they are not aware of adults then the adults cannot hear or see them. For example, notice how little children often 'hide' simply by covering their eyes with their hands.

37/46   Family and childhood

45 Atticus's arrival was . . .
What is the effect of saving this information until the end of the chapter? Notice how Scout's revelation suddenly adds drama and new meaning to something which has already happened in the novel. An important quality of the way the book has been written is the way events assume a greater and often a different importance, the further we read. We, the readers, constantly change our understanding of things which happen, just like the children do. This technique, of revealing new slants on past events as time goes by, is also a very skilful way of suggesting that the children are growing up.

In a way the book is almost circular in its construction; when you have finished reading the book, try going straight back to the start and beginning again – notice how the continuity of the story is still quite well maintained.

42/46   Aspects of style

Chapter 5

46 Dill was in hearty . . .
The humour here lies in the matter of fact way Scout relates the events and the straightforward way she deals with the situation. She still is very much the young child who feels that any argument can be settled with fists. We gradually see her grow away from this idea as we read further into the novel, and as she matures.

42/49   Scout
45/51   Aspects of style
44/51   Family and childhood

47 Miss Maudie hated her house . . .
Miss Maudie is a very sympathetic lady in the children's eyes. She allows them, within generous limits, a great deal of freedom in her garden, she talks to them in a friendly way, and she offers them cakes. She contrasts with the frightening, intolerant Mrs Dubose and the gossipy and rather empty-headed Miss Stephanie Crawford.

0/49   Miss Maudie

48 Apparently deciding that . . .
The strict sect of Baptists that Mr Radley belonged to had quite an influence in the South. Their narrow views about good behaviour added to the already intolerant atmosphere of Maycomb.

29/56   History
35/50   Prejudice
14/49   Religion

49 My confidence in pulpit Gospel . . .
Scout seems to grasp intuitively that these strict Baptists must be wrong in condemning Miss Maudie to hell for loving her garden. Scout appreciates Miss Maudie's goodness, and though she does not actually go about 'doing good' in the way some characters do, Scout senses that she is as worthy as those who do.

47/50   Miss Maudie
46/51   Scout
48/50   Religion

*Characters and ideas
previous/next comment*

49/52	Miss Maudie
48/53	Prejudice
49/117	Religion

50 Miss Maudie stopped rocking . . .

Miss Maudie has a firm core of common sense that makes her aware of the dangers of interpreting the Bible too literally. She fears that people like Mr Radley who believe they are right by strictly obeying the laws of their religion are hurting other people in the process. That, to her, is wrong. She says that these people are 'so busy worrying about the next world they've never learned to live in this one . . .'. Think about how accurately you could apply this criticism to Mr Radley, Miss Stephanie Crawford, Mrs Merriweather, or Atticus. Miss Maudie's comment is a central argument in the novel, and it is therefore especially appropriate that Harper Lee should show us so much of the children's education. We see that the children learn 'to live in this world' in a way which many adults cannot. The educational system in Maycomb, as represented by the children's teachers, seems to think that 'projects' and 'units' are a good preparation for 'this world'. Is this sort of attitude part of the problem which Harper Lee is drawing our attention to?

49/57	Scout
46/60	Aspects of style
46/76	Family and childhood

51 Miss Maudie stopped rocking . . .

Much of the humour in this book is at Scout's own expense, resulting from her childlike innocence. She does not understand the implication behind Miss Maudie's comment about whisky. One of the more interesting things which Harper Lee has done in writing this novel is to do with the way we are constantly reminded that events are seen from both an adult's and a child's point of view. This clever technique allows for some revealing contrasts of perception, for example at the trial, and it allows us to be a little more detached than if there were only one narrator (which, of course, in another sense is true).

50/68	Miss Maudie

52 'Do you think they're true, . . .'

Miss Maudie's nature is tolerant. She is critical of Miss Crawford for spreading rumours about Boo Radley. She looks upon Boo with sympathy and sees his fate as the tragic result of his father's strict following of religious principles.

38/55	Atticus
50/73	Prejudice

53 'You reckon he's crazy?'

Atticus's lack of hypocrisy is emphasized by Scout and agreed with by Miss Maudie, 'Atticus Finch is the same in his house as he is on the public streets'. This opinion is repeated later on in the book.

How many other people in the book are like Atticus, as regards their public and private behaviour? Look at the list below. For each person, or group, decide whether you think they would be the *same*, or *different*, in private as they are in public: Miss Maudie Atkinson, Miss Stephanie Crawford, Mrs Dubose, Mr Ewell, Mayella Ewell, Tom Robinson, the lynch mob (who appear in chapter 15).

Use the 'Characters in the novel' section on p 59 to help you get started with difficult ones, and browse through this commentary for further information and evidence.

43/111	Dill

54 'You all've gone crazy, . . .'

Why does Dill need to invent so many stories about his life? Notice how his fairy-tales are accepted quite tolerantly by Scout. How do you think Dill's home life differs from Jem's and Scout's? Is this the reason he invents his stories?

Characters and ideas
previous/next comment

55 'Son,' he said to Jem, . . .
Again Atticus tries to teach them about understanding. He urges them to look at what they have been doing from Boo Radley's point of view. What indication is there that Atticus is not as angry as he seems? Why does the author say that Atticus's 'mouth was surprisingly firm'?

53/60   Atticus
36/58   Understanding

Chapter 6

56 In the glare from . . .
In this strictly religious atmosphere what do you think would be the attitude to gambling? Look at Miss Rachel's reaction. Notice how the gentle humour of the book surfaces again in Scout's innocent misunderstanding of the reactions of adults – because they all 'stiffen' she thinks that 'the neighbours seemed satisfied' with Dill's outrageous explanation.

48/65   History

57 I began to feel sick.
Remember that Jem is four years older than Scout. He feels more mature and the shame of possible punishment from Atticus is a stronger pressure than the terror of the Radley Place. Scout does not understand this because she is still too young to regard punishment as something which affects her pride.

42/58   Jem
42/58   Scout

Chapter 7

58 Jem stayed moody and silent . . .
Scout is beginning to learn the lesson that Atticus has been teaching her. We do not yet know, however, why Jem is so moody. Scout assumes that it is a reaction to the terror of going back to the Radley Place at night, and alone. It is in fact another example of how we do not yet know all of the facts of the incident. When we do, our reaction will be very different from that of Scout's here.

57/59   Jem
57/59   Scout
55/91   Understanding

59 One afternoon . . .
How was Scout's behaviour in keeping quiet rewarded? Why was Jem so moody? What did the sewn-up trousers make him realize about Boo Radley? Who does he suspect is leaving the things in the tree? Why does this confuse him so much?

42/61   Boo Radley
42/61   Jem
58/60   Scout

Jem is going through the painful process of discarding youthful assumptions and ideas which he has now discovered to be quite wrong. This is also something which Atticus, amongst others, is trying to persuade the people of Maycomb to do – to discard their prejudice. In Jem's case the process is shown as being an inevitable part of growing up and becoming more mature. We are left to draw our own conclusions about the outcome of the trial, and what it implies about the 'maturity' of many of the people of Maycomb.

These developments are set as an ironic contrast to the children's state education, whose achievements (teaching Jem about the Dewey Decimal System, and enabling him to walk 'like an Egyptian') seem wholly irrelevant to the real business of growing up.

*Characters and ideas
previous/next comment*

60 The second grade was grim, . . .
Notice Atticus's dry but subtle humour as he gently corrects Jem's boastful
'facts' about Egypt.

55/66   Atticus
59/61   Jem
59/61   Scout

---

61 Jem looked from the girl-doll . . .
What goes Jem realize here that Scout does not? Notice again how the
narrator, although the same person as Scout, can make Scout appear
ignorant of the facts that the reader can guess at. This revealing style of
writing produces a very relaxed narrative which has a strong story-telling
flavour to it. It is an engaging approach to adopt, because people always love
to be told stories, and it holds the reader's attention very well. It is also a
very suitable style for a novel like this one, which moves from incident to
incident and which contains a lot of conversation mixed with description,
because it allows the writer to maintain the reader's interest.

59/66   Boo Radley
60/62   Jem
60/62   Scout
60/64   Aspects
        of style

---

62 Less than two weeks later . . .
Why does Jem not want Atticus to know where they had found these things?
Think about Atticus's reaction to them trying to make Boo come out. What
things has Scout still not connected?

61/63   Jem
61/64   Scout

---

63 Jem said nothing more . . .
Jem realizes that Mr Nathan Radley was lying about the tree. He had
deliberately blocked it up. Why should this move Jem to silent tears? Why
did Nathan Radley block up the hole in the tree? What could he hope to gain
by this? Jem seems to realize why Nathan did it; notice how much more he
understands than his sister. (Think about what Dolphus Raymond says
about the way people treat each other, and read 'Prejudice' on p 14.)

62/66   Jem

Chapter 8

64 Next morning I awoke, . . .
Look at the different kinds of humour in the snow episode. Scout's reaction
is funny because she over-reacts out of ignorance. There is the narrator's dry
humour about the effects of sin. Then there is amusement arising out of
Scout's innocent trust in all adult pronouncements. The information about
the Rosetta Stone is nonsense; this Egyptian stone inscribed with hiero-
glyphics had nothing at all to do with weather prediction!

62/66   Scout
61/69   Aspects
        of style

---

65 The telephone rang . . .
The smallness of the town is emphasized here. Look at the list of jobs
entrusted to the town's telephone operator. Touches like this continually
remind us of the inward-looking nature of the town, how isolated and small
it is. This process began 'with the nimble-wittedness of one Sinkfield', we
are told in chapter 13, who, although he saved the town from being built in
Winston Swamp, did not alleviate the town's isolation by getting it built
closer to the river. We discover that it takes a man two days to get from the

56/73   History

north end of the county to Maycomb in order to obtain 'store-bought' goods, which is surprising when we recall that Maycomb was the centre of government for the county.

66 I looked down . . .
What does Atticus mean when he says 'Looks like all of Maycomb was out tonight, in one way or another'? Who does Jem realize has put the blanket round Scout's shoulders? This is another example of real life contradicting the children's previously held beliefs. This happens several times: look, for example, at their meeting with Dolphus Raymond in chapter 20.

60/71	Atticus
61/67	Boo Radley
63/67	Jem
64/70	Scout

67 Jem seemed to have lost . . .
Why is Jem so anxious to tell Atticus all they know about Boo Radley? What does Jem now realize about Boo's character that Scout has yet to appreciate? How does she still see him? (Study her reaction when Jem mimics Boo approaching her with the blanket.)

66/207	Boo Radley
66/83	Jem

68 'Don't you worry about me, . . .'
How does Miss Maudie react to the destruction of her home? What does this tell you about her character? Why do you think Scout is surprised at her reaction? Miss Maudie seems to care more for her flowers than for her home; this is quite in keeping with her character, because of the things which she regards as being most important in life. Can you explain why the loss of her house does not upset her more than it does? (Read her character study on p 59 to give yourself some hints on this.)

52/125	Miss Maudie

Chapter 9

69 'You can just take . . .'
Look at the way the main episode of the book is introduced from Scout's point of view, and how it is introduced with confrontation. Why is this appropriate?

64/70	Aspects of style

70 'You can just take . . .'
Scout's frankness is funny. Notice her remark after her father's vain attempts to control her spirited behaviour, 'I soon forgot'. For a young hot-head like her, Atticus's lessons on tolerance fail to go very deep. He tries again (on the next page) to persuade her to fight with her head for a change.

66/74	Scout
69/72	Aspects of style

71 Atticus sighed.
The case of Tom Robinson is a matter of honour for Atticus. He knows he cannot win, but he cannot refuse to take it on for fear of losing his self-respect, the respect of his children and the respect of those townfolk whose opinions he values.

66/74	Atticus
0/90	Courage

		Characters and ideas
		previous/next comment

72 'Because I could never . . .'

Unlike the Boo Radley story where mystery and suspense are important elements, there is no suspense about the outcome of the Robinson trial. The narrator lets us know from the beginning the likely result. What effect does this produce? What is our attention held by if not the eventual outcome of the trial?

70/74	Aspects of style

73 'Atticus, are we going . . .'

Atticus can be so certain they will be defeated because he knows exactly what the status of the Negro is in the South. In spite of the abolition of slavery at the end of the Civil War the Negro remained a second-class citizen. He lived a separate life, in a separate part of town, received an inferior education, and had to take on the poorly paid jobs. Even in court he was not equal. In any case which involved a black man against a white man, the black man rarely won. This is why Atticus is so sure of failure.

65/82	History
53/82	Prejudice

74 'Come here, Scout,' . . .

Scout is beginning to remember to be reasonable and for a few weeks accepts being called a coward for the sake of her father. She is beginning to change, to grow up. As a reward she enjoys feeling noble for a while!

71/75	Atticus
66/76	Scout
72/76	Aspects of style

75 No amount of sighing . . .

Atticus has a great sense of duty towards his family. He refuses to break the tradition of Christmas even if some members of the family are tiresome to be with. This is important, because it demonstrates that even the tolerant Atticus has to work at keeping his feelings under control.

An important lesson, that the children learn as they get older, is that adults frequently have to do things which they might rather not do (for all kinds of reasons), and must do them properly. Examples of this are: defending Negroes, exposing liars, shooting dogs, and visiting dull relatives. These are of course all done by Atticus. See if you can identify who, as part of their increasing adulthood, has to: read to a viperous old lady, wear skirts, be polite, outgrow irrational fear, not use fists to settle arguments, break with the lynch mob, and accept her brother's courage (no, this last one is *not* Scout).

None of the above are applicable to Dill. Can you find any examples for him? What conclusions can you draw from what you find for Dill?

74/76	Atticus
51/76	Family and childhood

76 Rose Aylmer was . . .

Scout's growing up process leads her into the use of swear words. Atticus wisely ignores this latest trend and it is her uncle who reprimands her. Atticus's tolerant attitude towards his children comes in for a lot of criticism from the family, especially from Aunt Alexandra. Do you think Atticus is right to adopt the approach he does, or is he simply being a poor father and spoiling his children?

75/77	Atticus
74/77	Scout
74/79	Aspects of style
75/77	Family and childhood

77 Aunt Alexandra was fanatical . . .

Scout is obviously a tomboy. In fact if Jem wishes to insult her he accuses her of behaving like a girl – as in chapters 4 and 6. Notice the difference between Atticus and Aunt Alexandra in their attitude to Scout. Atticus lets Scout be

76/79	Atticus
0/100	Aunt Alexandra

as she is. Alexandra tries to make her dress and play as a girl, mistakenly believing that Atticus would somehow secretly prefer Scout to be that way.

| 76/78 | Scout |
| 76/79 | Family and childhood |

78 'If Uncle Atticus lets . . .'

Why did Scout attack Francis if she did not know the meaning of what he said?

| 77/79 | Scout |

79 I took a deep breath.

Children have a well-developed sense of fairness and Scout is angry with her uncle, not for the beating but because he did not take the trouble to listen to her side as well. Notice how Scout has come always to expect fair dealings because that is how Atticus has always treated Jem and her. Where is the humour here? Contrast the way Scout behaves with the way Uncle Jack behaves – is she telling him off? What has happened here to the usual positions of child and adult? Is there anywhere else in the novel where this situation occurs again? (Hint: look at the school scenes.)

77/80	Atticus
78/81	Scout
76/97	Aspects of style
77/80	Family and childhood

80 'Jack! When a child asks . . .'

Notice how well Atticus understands children. Firstly, he believes you have to be honest because children know when they are not getting a straight answer. Secondly, he selects from their behaviour the things that need correcting, like Scout's hot-headedness, and concentrates on those, and ignores those things that are probably best ignored, like Scout's new-found interest in swearing.

| 79/81 | Atticus |
| 79/92 | Family and childhood |

81 'That's not the answer,' . . .

Why does Atticus switch the conversation to the trial when he becomes aware that Scout is listening? He wants her to hear what he is saying, but he wants her to think that she is *overhearing* it, rather than being told it directly. Atticus is being very clever here, because we already know that Scout 'soon forgot' when he told her directly to do things (see comment number 70). What is Atticus worried about? Read carefully his conversation with his brother here.

| 80/82 | Atticus |
| 79/83 | Scout |

82 'It couldn't be worse, Jack.'

Atticus sets himself apart from the people of Maycomb. He does not share their prejudice when it comes to Negroes, although he is very realistic about his chances of changing their attitudes.

81/83	Atticus
73/83	History
73/95	Prejudice

83 'Right. But do you think . . .'

What is he afraid this trial might do to his relationship with his children? Whose influence does he fear they may fall under? What does he refer to when he mentions 'Maycomb's usual disease'? What do you think this is? (Read the section which follows that on 'Mockingbird' on p 14.)

82/85	Atticus
67/86	Jem
81/85	Scout
82/117	History

Chapter 10

84 When he gave us our air rifles . . .
Look at Miss Maudie's description of the mockingbird. As you learn more about the characters of Tom Robinson and Boo Radley, see how far you think that they fit this description.

85 'I mean young grown-ups.'
Why is this talk of Atticus's limitations (here and on the previous page) included at this point in the book? Does it diminish or increase his stature in the eyes of the children? In what way does it contrast with the stature Atticus acquires through later events? How do the children eventually come to regard Atticus?

86 The rifle cracked.
Why was Jem paralysed? Why do you think Atticus had kept his marksmanship a secret? Interestingly, Atticus is now not proud of something which, when he was younger, he was extremely proud of and took delight in. Now he takes no delight in it at all. Jem cannot understand this immediately, but realizes later that as people grow up their views of things change, providing they keep an open and tolerant mind about things.

87 'Maybe I can tell you,' . . .
Do you think that it is in keeping with his character that Atticus has not let his skill with a gun be known to his children? (Read 'Atticus' on p 59.)

88 When we went home . . .
Notice the difference between the two children now. Scout's reaction is the very reason why Atticus kept quiet about his talent. He did not want his children boasting about his ability to kill. Jem has grown up sufficiently to understand Atticus's reticence in this matter; in fact he is mature enough to admire Atticus's silence.

Chapter 11

89 Mrs Dubose lived alone . . .
Mrs Dubose appears to be a very unpleasant woman and the children, in their uncomplicated way, have clear feelings about her – 'Jem and I hated her'. However, she plays an important part in their growing up and by the time of her death they realize that people should not judge other people too quickly, or too superficially. They might have admired Atticus for all the wrong reasons if they had known about his skill with a gun. Similarly, they eventually learn that people they might never dream of admiring can have wholly admirable sides to their characters.

90 Atticus pushed my head . . .
The lesson that Jem and Scout are going to have to learn is that one has to do what is right whatever other people think. To do that sometimes requires considerable courage.

Characters and ideas previous/next comment	
0/161	Mockingbird
83/86	Atticus
83/88	Scout
85/87	Atticus
83/88	Jem
86/90	Atticus
86/89	Jem
85/89	Scout
88/91	Jem
0/92	Mrs Dubose
88/91	Scout
87/91	Atticus
71/92	Courage

91 I tried to explain to Atticus . . .
Atticus tries to cool their indignation at hearing their father being called names. He tries to make them understand that such language reflects badly on the person who uses it, not on the person it is directed at. This is a very difficult lesson for them to learn and later, when Mr Ewell spits in Atticus's face, the children are not the only ones to marvel at his cool reaction. Do you think that Atticus was really cool about it inside? Do you think Atticus ever experiences very strong emotions, or is it that he does have emotions like everybody else but he is also a man with very strong principles?

92 Jem opened the box.
Atticus tries to show his children the true meaning of courage. Mrs Dubose knew she was facing a very painful task in breaking her drug addiction, with little chance of success. Her courage lay in making the attempt. The fact that she succeeded is actually not all that important, it simply demonstrates that sometimes it is possible to win such battles. Was Mrs Dubose's victory a pointless one, do you think? How courageous is Atticus in taking on the impossible defence of Tom Robinson? Or do you think he is simply being stubborn for the sake of some silly principle, when he knows it will not make any difference in the end?

If you think Atticus is doing the right thing, isn't this terribly cruel and unkind to Tom Robinson? Everybody except the children knows what the outcome will be. Isn't Atticus just leading Tom on with false hopes? Wouldn't it be kinder to Tom to tell him that the case is hopeless? Is Tom Robinson's life being sacrificed just so that Atticus's conscience will feel better?

If you think that Atticus is really just indulging himself to impress everybody with how good a man he is, then what do you think Atticus should have done? Should Atticus, who has been appointed to defend a man in court, simply not bother just because that man is black? Wouldn't this be terribly unfair, especially as it is revealed that both the Ewells are probably lying about the whole matter of the rape?

Chapter 12

93 Jem was twelve.
Jem is growing up and Scout finds it difficult to accept the changes in him. Which of Jem's remarks indicates that he does not want their relationship to continue as before? Is Jem coming under pressure from the rest of his friends and classmates? Isn't this exactly what has happened, on a larger scale, with the inhabitants of Maycomb and isn't this exactly how intolerance and prejudice begin? Notice how even the tomboy Scout eventually has to conform to society's insistence on her behaving 'like a girl' and wearing a skirt. How does she manage to rebel against this imposition?

94 This change in Jem . . .
What evidence is there to show that Scout is bowing to the inevitable and beginning to throw off her tomboyish ways? What part can Calpurnia play in this development? Notice how Calpurnia invites her to come into the kitchen whenever she feels 'lonesome'.

Characters and ideas previous/next comment

90/104	Atticus
89/93	Jem
89/93	Scout
58/119	Understanding
89/0	Mrs Dubose
90/114	Courage
80/93	Family and childhood
91/99	Jem
91/94	Scout
92/94	Family and childhood
41/99	Calpurnia
92/96	Scout
93/98	Family and childhood

	Characters and ideas previous/next comment

95 'What you up to, Miss Cal?'
Jem and Scout are made to feel unwelcome by Lula because they are white. What point is the author making here about the racial prejudice in the South? Does it only work in one direction?

82/96   Prejudice

96 First Purchase was unceiled . . .
Scout watches what is going on with curiosity, comparing and contrasting this service with those in the church she usually attends. Notice how she is completely free from preconceived ideas about a 'Negro' church, and how this is reflected in the fascinated way she describes it.

94/99   Scout
95/98   Prejudice

97 Reverend Sykes closed . . .
Notice how we are again subtly and gradually informed of the facts of the Tom Robinson case. Because Scout is the narrator, all the information we receive must come to us within her hearing. How successful do you think this gradual and casual revelation of events is? Are there other ways in which the author could have let us, the reader, know the facts? Can you think of some reasons why these other ways might have been better? (Read 'Aspects of style' on p 11.)

79/102   Aspects of style

98 'He's just like our preacher,' . . .
The children's innocence shines through here. They have not yet absorbed the atmosphere of racial prejudice that hangs over the South in general, and Maycomb in particular. Scout does not understand that in terms of status in white society, all Negroes are regarded as being lower even than the Ewells.

94/99   Family and childhood
96/119   Prejudice

99 'I certainly am, Mister Jem.'
The visit to church marks an important point in their education. For the first time they understand that Calpurnia leads a 'double life'. From her they learn the important lesson that you cannot change people against their will. You cannot impose so-called 'better ways' on people: they have to want to change themselves. This is something which we see clearly demonstrated in the section of the novel which deals with the children's school education. The school teachers think that they can produce 'better' people simply by exposing the children to accepted Great Cultures, like that of ancient Egypt. We see from Jem's 'Egyptian period', where he spends a lot of time trying to walk sideways with his arms stuck out, how foolish this notion is. Incidentally, is there any significance in the fact that all the school teachers we meet are women? Think about the place women seem to occupy in Maycomb society.

94/123   Calpurnia
92/105   Jem
96/100   Scout
98/101   Family and childhood

Chapter 13

100 'Put my bag in . . .'
Why does Scout find it difficult to talk to her Aunt? What aspects of her aunt's character does she dislike? Notice how the children 'exchanged glances'.

77/102   Aunt Alexandra
99/101   Scout

101 The remainder of the afternoon . . .
Do you detect a new maturity in Scout's attitude to her aunt's stay? Notice

100/105   Scout

	Characters and ideas previous/next comment

her observation about lying. This is not the kind of thing we might have thought she would say, judging by her behaviour up to now. How would you have expected her to have answered Atticus's question?

102 When she settled in . . .

What evidence is there to show that the author is using a mocking tone when describing Aunt Alexandra? Look at the section containing the words 'let any moral come along and she would uphold it'. What overall impression do you get of Aunt Alexandra?

100/103 Aunt Alexandra
97/106 Aspects of style

103 'Speak to your Cousin Lily,' . . .

It has already been mentioned that family characteristics are important in Maycomb and no one clings to this belief more than Aunt Alexandra. She is particularly proud of the Finch family background and feels Jem and Scout should also be made to feel proud of it.

102/123 Aunt Alexandra
101/104 Family and childhood

104 Before bedtime I was . . .

Why does Atticus keep saying 'She asked me to tell you . . .'? What other signs are there that he does not really share his sister's belief in living up to the family name?

91/105 Atticus
103/107 Family and childhood

105 'Stop that noise,' Atticus said.

Scout and Jem are upset by the way Atticus is talking. In what way do they not want things to change?

104/106 Atticus
99/107 Jem
101/106 Scout

Chapter 14

106 'What's rape?' I asked him . . .

No doubt remembering what he told his brother (at the end of chapter 9) Atticus answers her question truthfully. The humour in the situation arises out of Scout's innocence and ignorance. She does not understand his definition but dismisses it and moves on to another query. By making Scout's question about visiting Calpurnia arise in front of Aunt Alexandra, the author is able to show us several revealing things at once. Firstly, we see how quick Aunt Alexandra is to impose her own views on her brother's household, and this demonstrates the extent of her prejudice and intolerance. Secondly, we see how quick all children are to respond to threats to their parents' authority, and this emphasizes Scout's youth and loyalty. Thirdly, we see what a difficult position all this places Atticus in, and this emphasizes the fact that he is not some superhuman figure who is able to be reasonable and fair because he is different from other people, but that his tolerance and lack of prejudice place a great strain upon him. Doing the right thing frequently involves making a sacrifice, and all real sacrifices hurt.

105/110 Atticus
105/107 Scout
102/110 Aspects of style

107 'They've been fussing, . . .'

Jem is beginning to understand things from an adult's point of view. He has some sense of the worry Atticus must be experiencing at the moment. Scout, who still sees the world very much as a child, has no idea that these undercurrents are present.

105/108 Jem
106/108 Scout
104/109 Family and childhood

Characters and ideas previous/next comment

108 His maddening superiority . . .
Why is Scout so resentful of the change in Jem? What does it show about Scout that she will not accept his new ways without protest? Remember their differences in age.

| 107/109 | Jem |
| 107/111 | Scout |

109 He had taken thirteen dollars . . .
What part of their childhood code has Jem betrayed, according to Scout? Why did he tell his father? Look at his concern that Dill should let his mother know where he is. Jem is growing up fast, and is becoming quite keenly aware of the way the adults involved would react to this situation. For example, Jem knows that whatever Dill's home background may really be like, his mother will probably be very worried by his sudden disappearance.

| 108/113 | Jem |
| 107/111 | Family and childhood |

110 'I'm not scared . . .'
Look at the way Atticus deals with Dill's unexpected arrival. He manages to be responsible, by informing Dill's aunt, without betraying the child's trust – he allows him to stay. Notice too, how the whole situation is managed by Atticus with humour and with no anger.

| 106/114 | Atticus |
| 106/112 | Aspects of style |

111 As Dill explained . . .
Contrast Scout, sure of Atticus's and Jem's affection, with Dill, a child who has everything in the material sense but who seems to be unwanted by his parents. Do you think this explains why Scout says on the next page that Dill 'preferred the magic of his own inventions'? Or is Dill's unhappy home background another one of these inventions? Why might Dill want to invent such a story?

54/149	Dill
108/116	Scout
109/113	Family and childhood

Chapter 15

112 It began one evening . . .
The use of a child as narrator increases the tension in the story. Whereas the reader understands the danger Atticus is in, Scout does not. The children sometimes see threats where there are none, and sometimes cannot see threats where we, the readers, can.

| 110/120 | Aspects of style |

113 They murmured and buzzed . . .
Did Jem really not hear his aunt? How does his attitude to the situation differ from that of his sister? Why is he afraid? Why is Scout not afraid? Is this to do with the different way they tend to see many things by this stage of the novel?

| 109/115 | Jem |
| 111/115 | Family and childhood |

114 'Do you really think so?'
Would Atticus's words about the truth have been welcomed by the group of friends that had come to see him? What were they more concerned about beyond the life of Tom Robinson? It is interesting that, for the most part, we never meet or get to know the people in Maycomb who are Atticus's friends and who support his actions. We tend to see and hear far more from the characters who are opposed to him. This increases our sense of Atticus's isolation and makes his behaviour stand out more vividly. Why might the author have wanted to do this?

110/115	Atticus
93/130	Courage
0/119	Violence

	Characters and ideas previous/next comment

115 There was a murmur . . .
Why did Jem call out to his father? Has he misinterpreted the situation? Look at the next page too. What quality does Jem still lack that Atticus has?

114/121	Atticus
113/116	Jem
113/118	Family and childhood

116 'The Ku Klux's gone,' said Atticus.
The gap between Jem and Scout is very wide. Jem worries about his father because he lacks Atticus's courage and knowledge of local people. Scout is too young to grasp the potential danger of the situation and so is not really concerned at all.

115/118	Jem
111/118	Scout

117 Our father had a few . . .
The comment about walking underlines the very puritanical, joyless view of life that most people held in Maycomb. We have already seen that according to some people in Maycomb, flowers are not to be enjoyed because they are sinful. Now it would appear that some people regard walks as something to be criticized unless they are taken for a particular purpose. Notice how the humorous way in which this viewpoint is expressed effectively ridicules the notion.

83/125	History
50/167	Religion

118 In the midst of this strange . . .
Why does Jem refuse to go home? What does he know about the present situation that Scout has failed to grasp?

116/132	Jem
116/119	Scout
115/124	Family and childhood

119 I began to feel sweat gathering . . .
Why does Mr Cunningham call off the lynch mob? How has Scout's innocent questioning brought him to his senses? Why does Scout begin to sweat?

118/120	Scout
98/120	Prejudice
91/120	Understanding
114/121	Violence

120 Walking towards the office . . .
How do we know that Scout still has not understood the situation? Look at Atticus's reaction after the men's cars had gone and compare it with Scout's question about whether or not they can now go home. What do you think Atticus might have been saying to Jem?

119/121	Scout
112/131	Aspects of style
119/122	Prejudice
119/124	Understanding

Chapter 16

121 We had come in quietly, . . .
The impact of the potential danger of the events at the jail does not hit Scout until later. What other dangerous situation comes to her mind at the same time?

115/123	Atticus
120/129	Scout
119/171	Violence

122 Everybody's appetite was . . .
Although Mr Underwood was prejudiced against Negroes he believed it was

37/131	Law

	Characters and ideas previous/next comment

the job of the law, and not the mob, to bring a person to justice. Hence his willingness to defend Atticus against attack. Mr Underwood, like Mrs Dubose, is another example of a character in the novel who we can at the same time admire and condemn. This is of course very true of most real people and it gives the characters, and hence the novel, a powerful sense of authenticity.

	120/123	Prejudice

123 Calpurnia was serving . . .
Notice the different attitudes that Atticus and Aunt Alexandra have towards Calpurnia. Atticus respects her and values her for her own self. He speaks frankly in front of her because he sees her as part of the family. To Aunt Alexandra she is just a Negro and therefore to admit in front of her that a white person is prejudiced against Negroes is just adding to the grievances of the Negroes.

121/124	Atticus
103/173	Aunt Alexandra
99/0	Calpurnia
122/126	Prejudice

124 'He might have hurt me . . .'
Atticus's observation reflects a crucial theme of the book. It takes a child to remind the adult that he is still a human being. In a mob a person might tend to act as a mindless member of a herd, but when he is made to recall that he is also a father and a friend, his reason returns and he sees the wrongness of his behaviour. By mentioning his son and talking about everyday problems Scout is able to bring Mr Cunningham back to reality, which helps him to see things from Atticus's point of view. This episode in the novel highlights the way in which in real life, people often behave differently under pressure from others than they do as individuals. This echoes what Miss Maudie says in the novel about Atticus being one of these people who is the same at home as he is on the public streets.

123/130	Atticus
118/129	Family and childhood
120/125	Understanding

125 'You goin' to court this morning?' . . .
How does Miss Maudie's attitude to the trial differ from that of the general population of Maycomb county? What does it say about her sympathy for Tom Robinson and her sensitivity towards people in general?

68/126	Miss Maudie
117/127	History
124/172	Understanding

126 Miss Stephanie Crawford came by.
Miss Crawford does not even have the honesty to admit her true motives for going into town. Consider whether Miss Maudie's sarcasm is justified. If you think Miss Crawford is lying about her reasons for visiting town, why do you think she is being so hypocritical? Who is she trying to deceive, and why? If she is trying to deceive Miss Maudie, surely she can see that it doesn't work? Is she trying to deceive herself?

0/166	Miss Crawford
125/166	Miss Maudie
123/127	Prejudice

127 We held off until noon . . .
Notice how important this trial is to the people of Maycomb. It is described as a 'gala occasion'. On the next page we see how the trial is being treated as a day's outing with picnicking in the square before the event begins. What does it say about the attitude of Southern people towards the Negroes that they will turn out in strength to witness what they know to be a foregone conclusion? Why have they bothered to come? We can perhaps quite easily understand that the black people have come hoping to see justice done. What have many of the white people come hoping to see?

125/165	History
126/128	Prejudice

	Characters and ideas previous/next comment	

128 'They don't belong anywhere.'

The depth of racial prejudice is emphasized again in the account we get here of Dolphus Raymond's life and the sad predicament of half-caste children. Given what we know already about the narrow and rigid views of the Southern whites, is Dolphus Raymond's expulsion from their community, even though voluntary, all that surprising?

Considering the way Southern society regards and treats them, how similar are half-caste children and characters like Dolphus Raymond, Boo Radley and Mayella Ewell?

127/129   Prejudice

---

129 'But how can you *tell?*'

Scout's freedom from prejudice is evident in the innocent questions she asks her brother.

121/130   Scout
124/133   Family and childhood
128/132   Prejudice

---

130 We knew there was . . .

Scout finds out that Atticus had not chosen, but was appointed, to defend Tom Robinson. She is puzzled because had she known, it would have been a good excuse to use when people were taunting her. Why didn't Atticus mention this to the children? In what way does this make him a more courageous man? Reread his conversation with his brother at the end of chapter 9.

124/144   Atticus
129/132   Scout
114/162   Courage

---

131 The Coloured balcony ran . . .

The narrator draws a very amusing picture of the judge, from the cleaning of his nails with his pocket knife to the chewing and regurgitation of his cigars. But behind the façade he is an astute and competent judge. He is another character whose real nature is different from the outside appearance we see on casual inspection. The novel is full of such characters, indeed it is the central theme of the novel that all people are such characters, and that a civilized society depends upon everybody learning to recognize, and act upon, this simple fact.

120/132   Aspects of style
122/137   Law

---

132 The Coloured balcony ran . . .

The children's admission to the balcony shows their lack of prejudice but it also solves some problems for the narrator in writing the book. From the courtroom floor Atticus cannot see the children. If he could he would probably send them out of court. The narrator (that is the author) needs them to be there. Why is their presence in the courtroom scenes essential for the success of the novel? (Read paragraphs 4 and 5 of 'Family and childhood', on p 13 for help with this.)

118/154   Jem
130/133   Scout
131/133   Aspects of style
129/134   Prejudice

Chapter 17

133 Jem's hand, which was resting . . .

Again Scout, as narrator, recalls incidents and observations that she did not actually understand. She misinterprets Jem's sudden excitement because she does not understand the necessity for calling a doctor in a rape case. Jem

132/136   Scout
132/136   Aspects of style

Characters and ideas
previous/next comment

does, and it is this contrast in the children's response which draws our attention to the matter more forcibly. It is difficult to think of a better way the author could have used to emphasize this revealing piece of testimony.

129/152	Family and childhood

134 All the little man on . . .

The only way that Mr Ewell is 'better' than his Negro neighbour is in the colour of his skin. This is the crux of the racial situation in the South at this time. A person's character does not matter, (in fact we learn later that Tom Robinson was an exceptionally kind and respectable man) merely the pigment of a person's skin. This one fact can pervert the whole course of justice.

37/135	Mr Ewell
0/146	Tom Robinson
132/137	Prejudice

135 'Yes? She was screaming?'

Notice the effect Mr Ewell's crude language has on the public in court. Why is there such an uproar? Why would Mr Ewell be pleased with this result, do you think?

134/138	Mr Ewell

136 'There has been a request,' . . .

Who could Judge Taylor be talking about here, particularly? How much of the rape case do you think Scout understands? Notice how, once again, interest is heightened by the narrator describing things that Scout (the child) cannot understand herself, but we can.

133/149	Scout
133/139	Aspects of style

137 'There has been a request,' . . .

Taylor rules his court with order and common sense. Scout is proof of his comment here. Although the outcome of the trial is unjust Judge Taylor and the court itself are not open to criticism. Both are fair. The fault lies with the prejudice of the people, particularly those sitting on the jury. As Atticus says in his summing up (chapter 20) the law can only function properly if the people allow it to, for 'a jury is only as sound as the men who make it up'.

131/141	Law
134/146	Prejudice

Notice how, later on, Scout wants to know why people like Miss Maudie never seem to get onto juries, because then she feels that justice would be done, and another side of prejudice is revealed – women were not allowed on juries at this time.

138 'You say you were at the window?'

How does Mr Ewell strike you here? Can you believe what he says about his property? Do you think anyone actually believes him?

135/139	Mr Ewell

139 Atticus was reaching into . . .

Notice how sarcastically the narrator describes Mr Ewell. Why is it funny to call him a 'fragrant gardenia'? On the previous page Scout refers to him as a 'red little rooster'. Why should this image be so appropriate for Mr Ewell?

138/172	Mr Ewell
136/158	Aspects of style

Scout's main concern, however, is that Mr Ewell was gaining an advantage over Atticus by carrying the sympathy of the crowd. Notice how it is the emotional appeal that seems to sway the crowd, not common sense.

What is the significance of Mr Ewell being left-handed? Notice how this fact, together with another fact which we learn about Tom Robinson, is suddenly produced at this stage in the novel. Why would letting us know these things earlier on somewhat have spoiled the book?

Chapter 18

140 In Maycomb County, it was easy . . .
Notice how Scout makes a distinction between Mayella and her father. However small her achievement is, she has tried to rise above the squalid conditions she lives in, and she therefore has some dignity. This is of course what hurts her so much when her lies are exposed by Atticus, the fact that she has betrayed herself. Mr Ewell also betrays himself but, because he has only the false dignity of the arrogant, he does not care – in fact he rather glories in it.

141 Mayella stared at him . . .
Judge Taylor's approach to Mayella is very sympathetic, even if he does find her hard to cope with.

142 Atticus got up grinning . . .
Mayella is quite a pathetic figure, so unused to being treated with routine courtesy that she feels that Atticus must be making fun of her when he calls her 'ma'am'. What does this tell us about the way she is normally used to being treated?

143 The witness frowned . . .
We must feel sympathy for Mayella here. What vision must she have of her own situation if she thinks that Atticus is making fun of her for having no friends?

144 When Atticus turned away . . .
Why is Atticus not triumphant in having caused doubt to be cast on Miss Mayella's testimony? Knowing his ability to put himself in other people's shoes, what do you think Atticus's opinion was of her? How similar is Atticus's reaction here to his reaction when he was obliged to shoot the mad dog?

145 'Jem,' I said, 'Mr Underwood's . . .'
What better recommendation could Judge Taylor have than Atticus's approval, despite his rather unusual habits which are described in this paragraph?

Chapter 19

146 'Tom, did you rape . . .'
The predicament that Tom found himself in sums up the whole position of the Negro in the prejudiced South. Whichever way he acted in this difficult situation would have made him look guilty in the eyes of white people. If he tried to defend himself against a white woman's advances the situation would be seen as being of his making, and therefore his fault anyway. If he ran, as he in fact did, it would be taken as an admission of guilt. He was in an impossible position.

Characters and ideas previous/next comment	
0/142	Mayella Ewell
137/145	Law
140/143	Mayella Ewell
142/0	Mayella Ewell
130/153	Atticus
141/147	Law
134/148	Tom Robinson
137/148	Prejudice

	Characters and ideas previous/next comment	

147 Atticus sat down.

Despite his casual manner the judge is very strict about the correct procedure. Link Deas had spoken out of turn, therefore he had to be called to order. Look on the next page to see how Atticus reacts to the judge's outburst. Atticus understands that there is a certain amount of acting in the judge's performance.

145/157   Law

148 'Tried to help her, I says.'

The inferiority of the Negro's position in the South is again underlined here. His status was so low that to show sympathy for a white person would be seen as gross impertinence. Negroes were not seen by whites as proper people, with feelings like them, and therefore equal rights. The whites would treat Tom's feeling sorry for Mayella in the same was as they would treat the suggestion that a dumb animal could feel sorry for a human being – they would regard it as an insulting suggestion. This explains Mr Gilmer's outrage at what Tom says.

146/0   Tom Robinson
146/150   Prejudice

149 This was as much as I heard . . .

Look at the difference in sensitivity between Dill and Scout. Dill is very disturbed by Mr Gilmer's tone, and although it can partly be explained by Scout's greater 'experience' of court matters (she expects the prosecuting lawyer to be harsh) nevertheless Dill, unlike Scout, has grasped the reality of the awful position that Tom Robinson is in.

111/152   Dill
136/150   Scout

Chapter 20

150 As Mr Dolphus Raymond was . . .

Notice how Scout has accepted the stories about Mr Raymond and how she judges him at first by his reputation. How does her opinion change as she talks to him? To which other characters in the book does this happen: that is, that the children change their opinions of them as time goes by?

149/158   Scout
148/151   Prejudice

151 Mr Raymond sat up against . . .

What do you think of Mr Raymond and his way of behaving? Is he not just feeding people's prejudice, by pretending to be odd? Would he not be better to set both black and white a good example by the way he lives in racial harmony? Do you think he has tried this and become disillusioned and so finds this masquerade easier for himself and for others? Although understandable, is Dolphus Raymond's solution essentially cowardly? Should we criticize him for this if we think him lacking in courage? If you think we should, would we be happy to adopt the same standpoint if Atticus behaved the same way? Or do we only 'forgive' Mr Raymond his 'cowardice' because it seems as though neither he nor anybody else has anything to lose by it?

150/152   Prejudice

152 'Then you just pretend you're . . . ?'

Mr Raymond reveals his secret to the children because he respects their innocence. They might understand because they have not yet been contaminated by prejudice. He is drawn to Dill because 'Things haven't caught up with that one's instinct yet'. Does Mr Raymond mean that Dill is still innocent of the ways of the world? Or does he refer to Dill's fantasy world, where real life never reaches?

149/170   Dill
133/160   Family and
            childhood
151/153   Prejudice

153 I had a feeling that I . . .
Like Atticus, Mr Raymond represents the views of the tolerant. He can see the 'hell white people give coloured folks'. He is not blinded by fear and hatred.

144/155	Atticus
152/155	Prejudice

154 Atticus was half-way through . . .
Jem, who has followed the trial with understanding, is confident that Atticus will win. This is because he is basing his judgment only upon what has gone on in the courtroom – on the actual evidence which has been presented. Atticus knows that the jury's verdict will be based more upon what they brought into the courtroom with them – their preconceived attitudes, their opinions, and the extent of their prejudice.

132/158	Jem

155 Atticus paused, then he did something . . .
Scout's humorous remarks about Atticus's state of dress indicate the exceptional nature of this case and the great efforts that Atticus is making to convince the jury, not just that Tom is innocent but that they must defy their ingrained traditions, their deepest prejudice, and stand up for a black man against a white. What tone of voice, what manner, is Atticus adopting to accomplish this task?

153/157	Atticus
153/156	Prejudice

156 'What was the evidence of . . .?'
Atticus sums up the crux of the trial. The time-honoured, rigid code of behaviour has been broken, and broken by a white person. It is this that Atticus is trying to make the jury face up to. They must have the courage to question their long-held beliefs. They must accept that the real world is not the way they have come to see it.

155/159	Prejudice

157 'One more thing, gentlemen, . . .'
Atticus points his finger to the nub of the issue, to the ideal of the book, which is that all men are equal in law.

155/162	Atticus
147/159	Law

Chapter 21

158 Calpurnia marched us home: . . .
This is another example of humour arising from Scout's innocence; she has no idea why Calpurnia thinks the trial is unsuitable for her but is just delighted that it is Jem who is getting into trouble for a change.

154/160	Jem
150/171	Scout
139/177	Aspects of style

159 'Nobody's moved, hardly,' . . .
The final comment about Judge Taylor's performance comes from a Negro himself. Reverend Sykes says that 'he was mighty fair-minded', even leaning towards their side a little. In this way, it is emphasized that the law itself is not wrong, but rather people's interpretation of that law, and this is influenced a great deal by their prejudices.

157/160	Law
156/165	Prejudice

*Characters and ideas
previous/next comment*

160 Jem smiled. 'He's not supposed . . .'
Jem is convinced that the evidence was clear-cut. He is completely confident that the verdict will reflect this. His growing up process is far from complete; he has still to learn about the complexities of human nature and their effect on human behaviour.

158/164	Jem
152/164	Family and childhood
159/168	Law

161 But I must have been . . .
The atmosphere in the court is as still as a cold February morning, when even the mockingbird is quiet. With their verdict the jury have killed the 'mockingbird' which is the reflection of their true selves, the value they place on that fragile thing called justice. The mockingbird here is a symbol not only of a gentle, harmless creature like Tom, but also of human values and of justice itself.

84/191	Mockingbird

162 What happened after that . . .
What does the recalling of the mad dog incident say about Atticus and the courage he has to summon up at this point? Why will Atticus need to be brave? Who does he have to face? What knowledge does he have to accept? (Bear in mind the consolation which Miss Maudie offers the children in the middle of chapter 22.)

157/163	Atticus
130/0	Courage

163 Someone was punching me, . . .
What does their standing up as Atticus passes say about the respect the Negroes have for him, even though the verdict went against Tom? Look at subsequent events at the Finch household, and the deliveries which are made.

162/164	Atticus

Chapter 22

164 It was Jem's turn to cry.
Atticus does not try to pretend otherwise to Jem that, in life, the just and right thing is not always done. Jem is devastated but Atticus realizes that he has got to learn the realities of life as it is lived in the South.

163/165	Atticus
160/167	Jem
160/165	Family and childhood

165 'Atticus–' said Jem bleakly.
Notice how Atticus acknowledges that only children seem to have been moved by the injustice of the case–the adults' view, as reflected by Aunt Rachel on the next page, is that there is nothing anyone can do to change matters. In her opinion Atticus is foolish and obstinate in thinking otherwise.

164/171	Atticus
164/174	Family and childhood
127/167	History
159/168	Prejudice

166 Miss Stephanie's nose quivered . . .
Notice again the contrast in attitude between these two women. Miss Crawford disapproves of the children being in court, especially on the Coloured balcony. Miss Maudie treats the children no differently from normal, and even bakes them cakes as a treat.

126/182	Miss Crawford
126/167	Miss Maudie

	Characters and ideas *previous/next comment*

167 'I simply want to tell you . . .'
Contrast Miss Maudie's view of religion with that of the strict Baptists earlier in the book. To Miss Maudie, Christianity is about loving one's neighbour and treating all men equally. She understands that at certain times in life a Christian is called upon to live up to these beliefs. She tries to give hope to Jem, by saying that there are good men in Maycomb who do try to be true Christians.

164/169	Jem
166/169	Miss Maudie
165/183	History
117/0	Religion

168 'We're the safest folks in . . .'
Miss Maudie makes an interesting point about the judge. He deliberately appointed Atticus because he knew that Atticus was the man who gave Maycomb the best chance of seeing justice done. Do you think that real progress has been made, and that Aunt Maudie's optimism is justified?

160/174	Law
165/169	Prejudice

169 'You think about that,' . . .
Like Atticus, Miss Maudie too is a realist and did not expect Atticus to win. But she sees signs for optimism in that at least he made the jury think for a long time. She sees that as a start. Because of his youth Jem cannot accept this yet; he does not realize that the ingrained attitudes and behaviour of people cannot be changed overnight.

167/170	Jem
167/181	Miss Maudie
168/175	Prejudice

170 'I think I'll be a clown . . .'
This is Dill's reaction to the injustice of the case. He is utterly disillusioned with people; he wants to separate himself from them and become a clown who laughs at them. Who else in his life has made him feel disillusioned with people? Who does Jem have to fall back on to help him through this difficult time, that Dill does not have?

152/0	Dill
169/171	Jem

Chapter 23

171 According to Miss Stephanie Crawford, . . .
Is Atticus's reaction to the assault predictable? (Read 'Atticus' on p 59 for more information.) Remember his advice to Scout, in the first couple of pages of chapter 9. Do you think Atticus expected Mr Ewell to react the way he did?

165/172	Atticus
170/174	Jem
158/177	Scout
121/172	Violence

172 But when he noticed us . . .
The children are naturally worried for their father's safety, because they believe Mr Ewell's threats. Atticus's hatred of violence makes him refuse to use a gun. He tries to make the children look at the situation from Mr Ewell's point of view. He is being extraordinarily reasonable in saying he would rather Mr Ewell vent his anger on him than on Mayella. Why might Mr Ewell possibly be angry at Mayella? Do future events prove Atticus to be right, or is his faith in the basic goodness of all men too great?

171/173	Atticus
139/0	Mr Ewell
125/189	Understanding
171/202	Violence

173 Aunt Alexandra entered the room . . .
For once Aunt Alexandra's interpretation of human nature is more accurate than Atticus's. In what future way does Bob Ewell try to seek revenge? (Look at chapter 28.)

172/174	Atticus
123/176	Aunt Alexandra

174 'But lots of folks have . . .'
Jem has still to grasp the complexities of adult life. Atticus explains the flaws in the legal system. Jem demands a simple, easy solution to them. He does not appreciate that laws can only be changed when enough people want them changed. Atticus warns Jem that things do not happen overnight. This is something which was said by Calpurnia earlier on in the novel, except that she was talking mainly about the level of general education amongst black people, and their resistance to learning.

173/175	Atticus
171/175	Jem
165/176	Family and childhood
168/175	Law

175 'If you had been on that jury . . .'
The law will not be changed until people's attitudes change. For as long as the colour of a person's skin determines a court's verdict, justice will not be done. Atticus upholds the ideal that every man is equal in the eyes of the law, but he also knows that, for the moment, the reality is often different.

174/176	Atticus
174/177	Jem
174/211	Law
169/176	Prejudice

176 'Don't be silly, Jean Louise,' . . .
Notice Aunt Alexandra's rigid views on 'family' again. The Cunninghams are not a suitable family for the Finches to associate with because of their inferior background; on the next page Aunt Alexandra calls them 'trash'. Her definition of trash contrasts with Atticus's, which you can find about half-way through chapter 27. We know the Cunninghams are honest and loyal people, so what does this say about the accuracy of Aunt Alexandra's judgment of others? Is she influenced more by people's social position or their personal qualities?

175/208	Atticus
173/186	Aunt Alexandra
174/177	Family and childhood
175/183	Prejudice

177 Jem was rearranging the objects . . .
In the depressing context of racial prejudice and social snobbery, the relationship between Jem and Scout forms a cheerful contrast. Scout is eager to say the right thing to please her brother, while he, developing a sense of maturity, tries to give her advice and consolation. Jem's pride in his chest shows that he is still a child at heart, and is amusing, as is Scout's wry comment at the bottom of the page.

175/179	Jem
171/178	Scout
158/181	Aspects of style
176/178	Family and childhood

178 'You know she's not used . . .'
Again we notice a child's sense of injustice. Scout is angry because the Cunninghams have been wrongly judged by Aunt Alexandra.

177/179	Scout
177/179	Family and childhood

179 Jem kicked off his shoes . . .
Jem's attempt to explain people's behaviour by splitting them into four categories is criticized by Scout. She recognizes the worth of people like the Cunninghams and explains their difference as merely the result of a lack of education. Jem believes that she is idealistic in thinking there is only one kind of people and that she will eventually become disillusioned, like him. Which side of the debate do you agree with? Which side do you feel that Atticus would support?

177/201	Jem
178/180	Scout
178/180	Family and childhood

Chapter 24

180 I didn't know whether . . .

Notice a new maturity in Scout's nature. She is learning to be considerate and put other people's feelings before her own. Look how she is careful to keep her dress clean in order to spare Calpurnia work. On the next page look at how she sits with the ladies, even though such gatherings fill her with 'vague apprehension'. She joins this gathering purely because she senses that if she does so her aunt will be pleased.

181 The ladies were cool . . .

Scout realizes that growing up takes a long time. She is embarrassed by her own frankness in revealing that she is still wearing her trousers under her dress! Notice Miss Maudie's loyalty to Scout; she does not join in the laughter at Scout's expense.

182 In the sudden silence . . .

Miss Crawford shows her unkind nature by trying to get a laugh at Scout's expense. She is referring to the children's presence at Tom's trial.

183 'I said to him: "Mr Everett," I said, . . .'

How can you reconcile the Maycomb ladies' sympathy for poor Africans with their callous disregard of the Negroes in their own midst? Why do they not see their own hypocrisy? Why is it easier to feel kinder towards people who are far away from you? Do we tend to have over-simplified views of distant places and events? It might be because we do not have all the facts, and because our own situation and prejudices are less likely to be involved. Do we tend to feel sorrier for the down-and-out we may see in town, or for the starving people we may see on posters of far-away places?

184 Mrs Merriweather faced Mrs Farrow: . . .

The contrast between the sympathy of the Maycomb ladies for the Africans and their lack of any understanding of the feelings of the Negroes is very apparent here. They expect the Negroes to forget about Tom Robinson and get on with their own business as usual. They are not prepared to accord black people any status at all, let alone equal status with themselves.

185 Mrs Merriweather nodded wisely.

Although Scout does not understand who the ladies are referring to here it is obvious to the reader that they mean Atticus. Far from appreciating that he was trying to ensure that Tom received justice they interpret his actions as merely 'stirring up' the negroes, and making them dissatisfied. Miss Maudie is angry with their criticism of Atticus and a moment of tension occurs in the room.

186 'His food doesn't stick . . .'

It is interesting to note the change in Aunt Alexandra. Her love for her brother and the knowledge of what it has cost him emotionally to go through with this case has separated her from the views and attitudes she would normally have shared with the other Maycomb ladies. Hence her gratitude to Miss Maudie for standing up for her brother. However, her polite dislike of 'atmosphere' makes her quickly divert the ladies from their topic of conversation by handing out the refreshments.

Characters and ideas previous/next comment

179/181	Scout
179/189	Family and childhood
169/185	Miss Maudie
180/187	Scout
177/199	Aspects of style
166/0	Miss Crawford
167/184	History
176/184	Prejudice
183/185	History
183/185	Prejudice
181/186	Miss Maudie
167/188	History
184/187	Prejudice
176/189	Aunt Alexandra
185/189	Miss Maudie

Characters and ideas previous/next comment

187 But I was more at home . . .
Although Scout has not fully understood the ladies' veiled comments about her father and the Negroes, she still concludes that she prefers the frankness of male company to the hypocritical talk of the ladies. Note the clever way the author suggests their hypocrisy with the abrupt ending of this paragraph and the start of the next, even though outwardly the women are actually talking about something else, the people in the North.

| 181/190 | Scout |
| 185/188 | Prejudice |

188 'Hypocrites, Mrs Perkins, born hypocrites,' . . .
There is truth in what the ladies of Maycomb say. Although the Northern states did not practise the same open policy of segregation as they did in the South in the 1930s, the blacks were still treated as second-class citizens in terms of education and job opportunities and they certainly did not mix in society with any degree of social freedom.

| 185/192 | History |
| 187/192 | Prejudice |

189 Atticus leaned against . . .
Notice the effect the news of Tom's death has on Aunt Alexandra. Her concern for her brother has brought her to stand in his shoes. She now sees the situation from his point of view and she is very moved. Maybe she realizes that 'background', as Miss Maudie points out on the next page, is not merely a matter of coming from a 'good' family, but is more a matter of having the courage to try to do what you feel is right even if it flies in the face of social custom. Miss Maudie's definition does of course allow that it would be possible for a black family to have 'background', whereas Aunt Alexandra's definition would never allow such a possibility.

186/190	Aunt Alexandra
186/0	Miss Maudie
180/197	Family and childhood
172/196	Understanding

190 'Calpurnia's on an errand . . .'
Scout appreciates that part of being a lady, and a valuable part too, is the ability to hide one's feelings and act normally in company. It is not always appropriate behaviour to be frank and open and it is not always hypocritical to hide what one really feels. We have already seen Scout learn this lesson when Atticus first asked her how she felt about Aunt Alexandra coming to stay with them. Scout's admiration for her aunt increases as she sees her pull herself together.

| 189/202 | Aunt Alexandra |
| 187/195 | Scout |

Chapter 25

191 'Don't do that, Scout.'
We see again the idea behind the mockingbird symbol; that it is wrong to kill creatures that do no harm. Jem prevents Scout from killing insects because 'they don't bother you'. The vision of man as a killer of harmless creatures is repeated in chapter 25 ('Maycomb was interested . . .'). When Tom Robinson's wife is told of his death she falls to the ground 'like a giant with a big foot just came along and stepped on her'. If you interpret the image to suggest that white society is the giant, how accurate is the metaphor?

| 161/194 | Mockingbird |

192 Maycomb was interested . . .
Look how the people of Maycomb receive the news of Tom's death. The repetition of 'typical' demonstrates how easily they slot the death into all their preconceived ideas about Negroes; as with the alleged rape, Tom's

| 188/193 | History |
| 188/195 | Prejudice |

Characters and ideas
previous/next comment

behaviour is interpreted to his disadvantage; it does not seem to matter what he does. They withdraw all human dignity from him even in the face of the callous way he was treated in death.

193 Mr B. B. Underwood was at his . . .
Notice the cynicism of the Maycomb people. They are unmoved by Mr Underwood's impassioned editorial. They see it as being written merely as a ploy to get Mr Underwood published in a more prestigious paper!

192/199   History

194 Mr B. B. Underwood was at his . . .
The image of the mockingbird is repeated in Mr Underwood's editorial and this underlines the wickedness of killing innocent creatures.

191/213   Mockingbird

195 How could this be so . . .
Scout finally wakes up to the truth about the trial of Tom Robinson. Until now she has taken the events of the trial at face value and has therefore been puzzled by the reaction of people like Jem and Dill. Now she understands why the whole affair is such a tragedy.

190/196   Scout
192/200   Prejudice

Chapter 26

196 The Radley Place had ceased . . .
What does Scout's reaction to the Radley Place tell you about how much she has grown up in the last year? How well has she learnt Atticus's lesson about walking around in the other person's skin if you wish to understand him?

195/198   Scout
189/214   Understanding

197 Perhaps Atticus was right, . . .
Do you think that the child's way of settling a disagreement is best? What advantage does it have over the adult way of behaving?

189/203   Family and childhood

198 Perhaps Atticus was right, . . .
Although Scout is beginning to mature it does not mean she understands or behaves entirely like an adult yet. She cannot comprehend the decision of the people of Maycomb, who have voted to re-elect Atticus to the state legislature, so she accepts the mystery without trying to unravel it. Can you understand why Atticus was re-elected? Wouldn't it be reasonable to expect that, after his 'lawing for niggers', the people of Maycomb would throw him out? Does this tell us something about the local citizens? Is Atticus's re-election a sign that Miss Maudie's optimism for the future is not altogether without cause?

196/200   Scout

199 I was forced to . . .
Notice the way the author satirizes the education system again. The gap between educational theory and practice is apparent when we see another good idea fail because of the teachers' lack of knowledge about the pupils' everyday lives and general background.

181/203   Aspects of style
39/0   Education
193/200   History

	Characters and ideas previous/next comment	

200 'Nothing, sir.' I went away, . . .
Scout becomes increasingly aware of the basic hypocrisy in people's thinking about the world. We've seen how uncomfortable she felt in the company of the missionary ladies who pitied the African tribe of Mrunas. Now she is faced with the strange contrast between those who condemn the persecution of the Jews but do not condemn the treatment to which the Negroes in their own town are subjected.

198/213	Scout
199/203	History
195/0	Prejudice

201 'Well, coming out of the . . .'
Notice how Jem still has not been able to come to terms with the knowledge that people are not as good as he once imagined. Has Atticus come to terms with this knowledge?

179/206	Jem

Chapter 27

202 'I don't like it, Atticus, . . .'
Aunt Alexandra senses that Bob Ewell is paying back everyone whom he felt was against him at the trial. The suspense is built up about what might happen to Atticus or his family. Aunt Alexandra is not as optimistic as Atticus is about their family's chance of escaping Bob Ewell's revenge.

190/0	Aunt Alexandra
172/209	Violence

203 Aunt Alexandra was thriving.
The narrator gently satirizes the attitudes of the ladies of Maycomb. 'They had so little sense of family that the whole tribe was one big family' is mocking the exaggerated importance that the people of Maycomb attached to family name. Would everybody in the South have been better off if, like the Mrunas, they could see themselves as belonging to 'one big family'?

199/205	Aspects of style
197/0	Family and childhood
200/204	History

204 Maycomb was itself again.
The National Recovery Act was introduced by President Roosevelt, but was seen not to be helping the country to recover from the economic depression. It was therefore cancelled (repealed) by the Supreme Court (the nine old men).

203/0	History

205 When Halloween came, . . .
Notice how the situation is being arranged. We are being warned that something might happen. Atticus and Aunt Alexandra have declined to go to the pageant, therefore the children will return home alone. Aunt Alexandra has a feeling something might happen. We are left wondering what this could be, and expecting the worst.

203/207	Aspects of style

Chapter 28

206 Mrs Merriweather seemed to have . . .
Notice how tactful and diplomatic Jem is becoming. He is rivalling his father in his ability to say the right thing at the right moment.

201/0	Jem

207 'Yes sir.' I retreated.
Scout is very incurious about this stranger on their porch. Of course she does not yet know that it is Boo Radley. Her lack of interest is ironic, because for the last two years she has been anxious to see him and now she does not realize that he is standing on her porch!

Characters and ideas previous/next comment	
67/210 205/0	Boo Radley Aspects of style

Chapter 29

208 Aunt Alexandra got up . . .
A strong note of sympathy is struck here for Atticus. The attack on his children has affected him deeply and now he has to endure the further shock of Bob Ewell's death. Whom does he think has killed him?

176/209   Atticus

209 'He was out of his mind,' said Atticus.
For one so wise, Atticus has made a great error of judgment over Bob Ewell. He has miscalculated the lengths to which Bob Ewell would go in search of his revenge. His faith in people has, in a sense, let him down. Do you agree with Heck Tate's view that 'some kind of men you have to shoot before you can pay hidy to 'em'?

208/211   Atticus
202/0   Violence

210 He was still leaning . . .
Look at the description of Boo Radley. Although he is as pale as a ghost, he does not have any of the frightening characteristics that the children once furnished him with. He is not a rampaging monster of the night; in fact he is very shy.

207/212   Boo Radley

Chapter 30

211 Atticus walked to the corner . . .
Atticus wrongly believes that Jem killed Bob Ewell, but he wants there to be no cover-up. He wants the facts dealt with fairly in a court of law, to satisfy his own self-esteem and that of his children. But for a second time he has made a serious error of judgment. As Heck Tate points out later, with his injured arm and his lack of weight Jem could not possibly have stabbed Bob Ewell. Interestingly, this is the second time that an injured arm has been used to show that someone could not have committed a crime against a member of the Ewell family.

209/0   Atticus
175/212   Law

212 'I never heard tell that it's . . .'
Who is the sheriff protecting by insisting that Bob Ewell fell on his knife? What do you think of the arguments put forward by him for not bringing Boo Radley into the limelight of a public courtroom? Do they rely for their weight on legal considerations, or on humanitarian considerations to do with the understanding of others' situations?

210/0   Boo Radley
211/0   Law

213 Atticus sat looking at the floor . . .
Scout understands the sheriff. She likens Boo Radley, an innocent figure who has only done good, to a mockingbird who does no harm but merely sings. Within this one image the two strands of the story are linked, because Tom Robinson was also likened to a mockingbird.

200/214   Scout
194/0   Mockingbird

Chapter 31

214 We came to the street-light . . .
Notice how much Scout has grown up. She is ceasing to be the child who sees everything from a selfish point of view. She finally has taken Atticus's lesson to heart; as she comments on the next page, 'you never know a man until you stand in his shoes and walk around in them'.

213/0   Scout
196/0   Understanding

Characters in the novel

Aunt Alexandra

Aunt Alexandra is Atticus's younger sister who comes to stay in order to give Scout and Jem some feminine guidance. She seems quite disagreeable at first with her 'river-boat, boarding school manners'. She attempts to make Scout more lady-like, curbs the children's freedom and refuses to allow them to mix with the Cunninghams because the latter have not the right kind of background. She is at odds with Atticus about the way he is raising the children and thoroughly disagrees with him defending Tom Robinson. We can guess at her definition of the 'right' sort of people by looking at her attitude in chapter 13. Scout never understands her Aunty's preoccupation with 'family' and 'heredity' – what Scout amusingly calls 'other tribal groups'. Aunt Alexandra mellows after the trial however, when she sees what a strain the events are placing on her brother. Scout looks on her Aunt with new respect when she sees her behaving with great self-control at the missionary circle tea-party. Aunt Alexandra, in her turn, seems to come to regard Scout with more affection. She is particularly kind to Scout after Bob Ewell's attack.

Miss Maudie Atkinson

Miss Maudie is the children's favourite neighbour. She is popular with them because she treats them with kindness and respect. She genuinely likes their company, bakes them cakes and, most importantly, does not talk down to them. She is a very individual character, who shows her courage by holding views different from those held by other people in Maycomb. When criticized by the strict sect of Baptists for growing flowers, she matches their biblical quotations with others from the same source. She is quite philosophical about losing her house in the fire and cheerfully carries on with life. She is very critical about people's motives when they go to watch the trial, calling it a 'Roman carnival'. She knows the verdict of the trial to be inevitable, but she sees grounds for optimism, even though she thinks the verdict is wrong. She explains to the children that a small step on the path to true justice has been taken. She has a sharp tongue and is not slow to use it when faced with the hypocrisy of the ladies at the missionary tea. Scout admires and respects her for this. With Atticus, she represents the voice of reason amongst all the fears and prejudices of the town. Her attitude towards hypocrisy can be guessed from the way she reacts in chapter 24, where Mrs Merriweather is criticizing Atticus, when she acidly says 'His food doesn't stick going down, does it?'

Atticus

Atticus Finch, a widower of 50, is the father of Jem and Scout and with the help of Calpurnia, the cook, is raising the children on his own. He stands out as a man of reason and courage. In many ways he is central to the whole point of the novel. In the face of the prejudice and strong emotions of the people of Maycomb he tries to make his own children see that it is better to use one's head than to resort to fists or, even worse, to guns. His bravery in defending Tom Robinson, knowing the likely outcome of the trial, and the lack of sympathy from most of the townspeople, are both considerable. He is driven by a strong belief in the equality of men before the law, and although he fails this time to gain a just verdict it does not diminish his faith in the law for, as he remarks in chapter 11, 'before I can live with other folks I've got to live with myself. The one thing that doesn't abide by majority rule is a person's conscience.'

His children are disappointed that Atticus doesn't play football or poker, and that he neither drinks nor smokes. Atticus is described as old and short-sighted. On the other hand, he is an expert marksman and a man to be relied upon. He is chosen to deal with the mad dog and his advice is sought about the dangers of moving Tom Robinson to Maycomb jail. The people who matter in Maycomb hold Atticus in very high regard.

Atticus is subjected to criticism from his brother and sister because of the way he brings up his children. Although he gives Jem and Scout considerable freedom he demands high standards of courtesy, honesty and good manners from them. He is very fair with them and will always listen to both sides of any argument. He represents the voice of truth and fairness in the community – notice Dolphus Raymond's opinion of him in chapter 20. Miss Maudie says of him, 'We trust him to do right'. Atticus's philosophy of life is expressed early on in the novel, in chapter 3, where he says to Scout 'You never really understand a person until you consider things from his point of view . . . until you climb into his skin and walk around in it.' Despite his great virtues he is not unapproachable and is a popular man with a very keen sense of humour, which makes him human and likeable. But Atticus is not perfect. His faith in the goodness of man leads him to underestimate Bob Ewell, with almost fatal consequences. His other mistake, in thinking that they don't have lynch mobs in Maycomb, might also have resulted in death.

Mrs Dubose's courage is admired by Atticus, but she is an unlikeable person – other characters in the book are likeable but lacking in courage, Dolphus Raymond, for example. Atticus is perhaps the only adult we meet who is both courageous and likeable.

Calpurnia

Calpurnia is more than the family's cook. She is a replacement mother. Her firm control over Jem and Scout causes Scout, particularly, to resent her when she is small. Atticus trusts and supports Calpurnia entirely. When Aunt Alexandra wants to get rid of her he is firmly against it. Calpurnia is intelligent and full of common sense and she is one of the few Negroes in Maycomb who can read and write. Calpurnia leads a 'double life', partly amongst white people, partly at home with her fellow Negroes. The children, when they become aware of this dual existence, are surprised that she talks differently amongst her own people. Calpurnia is very down to earth in her explanation of this. People have got to want to be educated themselves. You cannot force them. If they do not want it there is no point flaunting your own education.

Contrast the way Calpurnia is treated with the way the hypocritical Mrs Merriweather treats her maid, Sophy; in chapter 24 we get some insight into this when, after Tom's trial, she remarks that she told Sophy 'you simply are not being a Christian today. Jesus Christ never went around grumbling and complaining'.

Miss Stephanie Crawford

She is a neighbour and quite the opposite of Miss Maudie. She embodies all the worst aspects of Maycomb people. She is bigoted, prejudiced, unkind and a gossip. She was the first to fill the children with all the wild notions about Boo Radley. She teases Scout unkindly at Aunt Alexandra's tea party.

Dill

Dill, real name Charles Baker Harris, is nearly seven at the start of the book and is the friend of Jem and Scout. He comes to stay each summer with his Aunt Rachel, a neighbour of the Finches. They like his ability to make up stories and think up imaginative games. It is he that suggests making Boo Radley 'come out'. It becomes apparent that his liking for fantasy hides an unhappy home life. We get a good insight into this towards the end of chapter 14, as Dill describes the way his parents ignore him. Although he is bought all that he could wish for he is unloved and feels unwanted. Dill is very upset by the trial of Tom Robinson and the outcome leaves him feeling very disillusioned about adults. Jem sees injustice as a challenge and says he wants to become a lawyer, but Dill thinks it is pointless to fight against it. He wants to become a clown when he is older and just laugh at grown-ups. In chapter 22 Aunt Alexandra calls Dill 'cynical', which means always believing the worst of others. To what extent do you think that the children's different attitudes and reactions can be attributed to their different home backgrounds, the way they have been brought up, and the way they have been treated by their parents? Could these things explain the attitudes and behaviour of other people in the novel – Mayella Ewell, for example?

Mrs Dubose

Mrs Henry Lafayette Dubose is a neighbour of the Finches who frightens the children with her unkind remarks. She appears and dies in one chapter (chapter 11) and through her the children learn an important lesson about courage. Over the years she had become addicted to morphine, which she used as a pain-killer because of her illness, but she struggled at the end of her life to free herself from the addiction, even though it would make no difference to her coming death. Without realizing it, the children help her to achieve her important personal victory.

Mr Ewell

Bob Ewell is a drunkard, almost certainly a cruel father and a liar. He is a poor farmer but, unlike the Cunninghams, he does not try to live with dignity; instead he lives on relief cheques issued by the State. His children are filthy and half-starved because he spends his relief money on drink. He is violent towards his children and when he tries to turn one particular bout of violence to his advantage by accusing Tom Robinson of rape, he finds that although Tom is found guilty, nobody really believes his story. Whereas he thought he would gain some public sympathy he gains only ridicule. This sets him on the path of revenge, which leads to his own death.

Mayella Ewell

The 19-year-old daughter of Bob Ewell, it is Mayella's deceit that brings Tom Robinson to trial. Although perhaps she cannot be forgiven for this vicious lie, both Atticus and Scout feel sympathy for her because they know she is the victim of her father's cruelty and the terrible poverty in which she lives. Scout senses that she must be very lonely and we can perhaps understand her responding to the kindness of Tom Robinson, who was probably the only person who had ever been considerate towards her.

Mayella's position in white society is neatly summed up by Aunt Alexandra, who describes the family as 'trash'. In chapter 19 Scout reflects that 'She was as sad, I thought, as what Jem called a mixed child: white people wouldn't have anything to do with her because she lived among pigs; Negroes wouldn't have anything to do with her because she was white'.

Jem

The story begins when Jem is 10 and finishes when he is 13. The development of his character is traced as he approaches adolescence. At first Jem enjoys normal childhood pursuits like playing football, inventing games, and amusing himself with his friends. Scout is regarded as acceptable because she is a tomboy. As the story unfolds Jem becomes more moody, less willing to join in games with Scout and Dill, preferring to be on his own. He is milder tempered than his sister and more sensitive to other people. Jem is four years older than Scout and this is reflected in his attitudes and reactions. The author uses the clever device of allowing us to see Scout trying to guess at Jem's thoughts on several occasions; this reveals a great deal about both Scout and Jem. A good example of this occurs in chapter 7, when the children find the two carved soap figures in the Radley's tree.

Only on one occasion does Jem explode into anger – when he cuts off the tops of Mrs Dubose's camellias. As a result of this incident he learns a lot about personal courage.

Tom Robinson's trial is also a very significant event in Jem's growing up. He is devastated by the unjust verdict and it takes him a long time to come to terms with the imperfections of people. At the same time his awareness of the feelings of others increases and he finally understands that Boo Radley stays indoors because he wants to, not for all the sinister reasons the children had imagined earlier. Jem develops a keen sense of responsibility, which is shown when he seems to break the childhood code of secrecy and informs Atticus of Dill's presence. Towards his sister he becomes more protective and develops a tactfulness and a way with words that is reminiscent of Atticus.

Boo Radley

Arthur Radley, or Boo as the children call him, is a figure of fear and mystery at the beginning of the story. Locked in the house by his father for stealing a vehicle and then resisting arrest 15 years before, when he was 18, he becomes a monster, ghost or 'haint' in the minds of the children. ('Haint' probably comes from the French 'hanté', which means haunted.) The children learn that when he was 33 years old he calmly stabbed his father in the leg with a pair of scissors and had to be locked up in the court-house basement. The community's exaggeration and fear enlarges his activities to including poisoning pecan nuts in the schoolyard, eating cats and squirrels raw, terrifying Miss Crawford by staring through her window at night and killing azaleas by breathing on them.

Through various incidents in the story, Boo emerges as being in fact a very different sort of person from the one the children imagine him to be. When items appear in the tree outside his house, the children eventually realize he is leaving them gifts. When Jem tears, and has to abandon, his trousers on the Radley fence they reappear mended. When Scout is watching the fire at Miss Maudie's house Boo covers her shoulders with a blanket. Boo's greatest act of kindness is in coming to Jem and Scout's aid when they are attacked by Bob Ewell, even though this involves him in killing a man with a knife. It is only then that they actually meet Boo for the first time. He is very different from the monster of their imagination, or that described by Stephanie Crawford in chapter 1. He is a gentle, quiet man, who is shy in company.

Tom Robinson

Tom Robinson, the Negro accused of raping Mayella Ewell, is a married man of 25 who becomes a victim of the society in which he lives. Although he has a criminal record and has served a prison sentence in the past, he is a respectable, honest family man who gets into trouble simply because he feels sorry for a white woman. Although it is proved impossible that he could have attacked anyone in the way his accusers describe (because of his withered arm), he is found guilty because people can not bring themselves to accept the fact that a white woman desired a black man. Chapter 19 details Tom's fatal error and the reaction of others to it. In many ways Tom is quite like Boo Radley – we find out very little about him; things happen to him but he remains something of a mystery. Look at chapter 19 and see if you can work out what he may have been thinking from the time when he approached the Ewell's place on 21 November (the date of the alleged rape) to when he ran away from Bob Ewell.

Scout

The story is narrated by Scout, who is six at the beginning and nine when the story ends. The language of the book is very adult in style, because Scout is recounting memories of her childhood. Interestingly, the book is set in the 1930s and Harper Lee would have been seven in 1933 – she is therefore contemporary with Scout. Scout is a lively, intelligent, astute girl who prefers boyish activities. She has a strong will and a hot temper which gets her into trouble with adults. She dislikes school intensely and lets her feelings be known to the teacher. She has a very close relationship with her father, who is always trying to make her use her head instead of her fists. Before the trial she is subjected to teasing and taunting from the other children because Atticus is defending a Negro. Her instinctive reaction is to fight back but swallowing her pride she obeys her father and refuses to retaliate. Her wild behaviour and frank speech offend Aunt Alexandra who feels she must become more 'ladylike'. Scout resists these attempts to make her more feminine, preferring the openness of male company to the sly insinuations of her aunt's associates. She learns to value the ability to hide one's feelings, however, and finally admires her aunt's self-control in front of her friends. We see Scout's character change as she begins to look at things from another person's point of view. She learns to understand the feelings of Boo Radley and of her aunt too, and also to respect the changes in Jem. She has a great sympathy for Mayella Ewell and for her friend Dill. She is quite without prejudice, and has a great curiosity about Calpurnia and the way she lives. She is very spontaneous and open with other people and it is these qualities which deflate a very nasty situation outside the courthouse when Atticus faces a lynch mob.

Having a child's mind and approach to life is often seen in the novel as being an advantage; the situation outside the courthouse is a good example of this. The children learn by experience that adults are not always right, and the trial is the most powerful example of this. Scout illustrates the importance of developing an open and unprejudiced mind of one's own. She decides very early in life that no matter how other people seek to divide up the human race into different sorts or types of people, there is really 'just one kind of folks. Folks.'

What happens in each chapter

Chapter 1   The story is narrated by a young girl who lives with her father, brother and their cook in Maycomb, a small town in Alabama in the south of the USA. The story relates events from the time the narrator was six until she was nearly nine. In this chapter we meet Dill, their friend with whom they share the adventures and we are told about the Radley family, the mystery surrounding their son Arthur (whom the children call Boo) and the children's attempt to make him come out of his house. These activities take place in the middle 1930s in a town which is small, hot and 'tired', where the people are religious but narrow-minded and intolerant of those who do not conform to their very rigid code of social behaviour, and where everybody knows everyone else because the same families have lived there for generations.

Chapter 2   Scout's first day at school does not go as smoothly as she imagined it would. She is scolded for already knowing how to read and write, and admonished for speaking out in Walter Cunningham's favour. The morning ends with her standing in the corner, her hands slapped. The author is gently making fun of an education system which is in favour of new methods but which takes no account of an individual's own abilities. The difficulties of being an outsider in a small town like Maycomb are emphasized when, for example, Miss Caroline the new teacher is given a very hard time.

Chapter 3   Burris Ewell arrives for his once-every-year day of attendance at school, and Miss Fisher finds out about his 'cooties'. Walter Cunningham visits the Finch home for lunch and Scout is taught an important lesson by Calpurnia about politeness to guests. Scout also learns about the position of the Ewells in Maycomb, a family for whom the normal rules of behaviour are relaxed, in order to shield the Ewell children from some of the bad habits of their 'contentious' father. Most importantly, Atticus tries to teach his children tolerance, and tries to make them learn to see things from the other person's point of view.

Chapter 4   A whole year passes which leaves Scout very disenchanted with school life. The mystery of the Radley place deepens as the children begin to find small gifts (like the chewing gum) left in the tree outside. As yet, Scout does not suspect that they originate from Boo. Dill arrives and they invent a new game re-enacting the drama of Boo Radley's life. Scout rolls inside a tyre into the Radley's garden. Scout is apprehensive, partly because she senses that Atticus disapproves of their game, partly because unknown to the boys she heard laughter coming from behind a shutter at the Radley Place.

Chapter 5   Scout, having been edged out of the boys' games for a while, spends her time with Miss Maudie. She is their friendliest neighbour, kind and generous to the children. She is critical of the local gossip, Miss Crawford, and of religious bigots like Mr Radley. She has tremendous sympathy for Boo Radley, whom she feels has been cruelly treated. The children's last attempt to communicate with Boo fails when Atticus catches them using a pole to push a note through one of the Radley's shutters. He forbids them to torment Boo any more, and urges them to look at their behaviour from Boo's point of view.

Chapter 6   Despite Atticus's ban, the children try a final time to make contact with Boo Radley. They go at night and catch sight of a shadowy figure in the Radley backyard. Before they can discover its identity the sound of Nathan Radley's gun frightens them off the premises. In the escape Jem loses his trousers on the barbed wire. It takes all Dill's ingenuity to make up a plausible reason for their disappearance—he says that he beat Jem at strip-poker. Jem, fearing Atticus's anger more than Mr Radley's shotgun, goes back that night to find that his trousers have been mended, and have been left hanging neatly on the fence.

Chapter 7   Jem appears to be more sensitive and mature than his sister. He seems to guess that Boo Radley repaired his trousers and hung them on the fence. He also suspects that the gifts in the tree (some twine, and soap carvings of two figures) are from Boo Radley. Jem's suspicions are sadly confirmed when Boo's brother Nathan cements up the hole before he can write a thank-you note. The knowledge that Nathan wants to prevent any friendship between Boo and the children reduces Jem to tears. Scout has not understood the origin of the presents or the significance of the cement, yet the narrator (the older Scout) is able to convey Jem's understanding to us at the same time as she illustrates Scout's ignorance.

Chapter 8   Mrs Radley dies. The children see snow for the first time. The winter is the coldest since 1885. The children make a snowman which is a caricature of Mr Avery (a 'morphodite' as Miss Maudie calls it) but Atticus, with his usual tact, makes them change its shape so as not to offend Mr Avery. While the children watch the fire which burns down Miss Maudie Atkinson's home, someone puts a blanket around Scout's shoulders. It is realized later that this must have been Boo Radley. For Jem, this act of kindness clinches Boo Radley's true nature and he pours out all their dealings with Boo to his father. Finally, Scout sees Boo as a kind man, not the monster which they had imagined. Miss Maudie accepts the ruin of her home philosophically.

Chapter 9   Atticus knows that defending Tom Robinson will have a deep affect on his family. He already sees this with Scout; he has to persuade her not to let the insults against him bother her (Cecil Jacobs taunts her, for example). Uncle Jack (Atticus's brother) arrives for Christmas and Jem and Scout get air-rifles from Atticus. They all go to Finch's Landing for Christmas Day. Scout manages to control her behaviour until she meets her cousin Francis, but he provokes her and she gets into a fight with him. She is punished by Uncle Jack but unjustly, she feels, because her side of things has not been heard. When the children have gone to bed, Atticus explains to his brother that he is worried that Scout will not be able to cope with the pressure that the family will be under during the time he is defending Tom Robinson—during this conversation Atticus knows that Scout (who came down for a drink of water) is listening from the hall.

Chapter 10   The chapter begins with the children explaining that they are disappointed with their father's accomplishments as compared with those of their friends' fathers. The chapter ends with them feeling deep pride and admiration for him. Atticus shows courage and skill in shooting the mad dog. Jem is mature enough to understand that he has kept his marksmanship a secret from them out of modesty and out of an awareness of the responsibility of such a skill. It is in this chapter too that Atticus mentions the mockingbird and explains that it is wrong to kill something that does no harm, and only gives pleasure by its song.

Chapter 11   Quite out of character Jem loses his temper with their outspoken, cantankerous old neighbour Mrs Dubose. In retaliation for the names she calls his father, he cuts off the heads of her camellias. Atticus is angry that Jem should have behaved in such a way to a sick old lady. As punishment he has to read to her for a month. Scout goes with him and realizes that these reading sessions increase daily in length. On Mrs Dubose's death Atticus explains the important part Jem and Scout have played in helping Mrs Dubose overcome her morphine addiction. He tries to show them that they have been witnessing true courage at work; despite her rudeness Atticus has great admiration for Mrs Dubose. Atticus explains that true courage is a matter of facing up to a challenge, it is not simply a man with a gun.

Chapter 12   Jem is growing up and to Scout's disappointment is unwilling to play with her any more. While Atticus is away Calpurnia takes the children to her church. It is a memorable experience for them. They meet hostility from one person, Lula, but the majority are welcoming. Scout attends the service with interest and notices the many similarities with their own church. They learn more about the nature of Tom Robinson's alleged offence and the situation of his family. They also see Calpurnia with new interest, and they enquire about her background and her relations with the other blacks. A collection is made in the church for Helen Robinson and her children. Calpurnia tells Scout that Tom Robinson is accused of raping Mayella Ewell. Aunt Alexandra arrives.

Chapter 13   Aunt Alexandra comes to stay indefinitely because she feels the children need feminine influence as they face their crucial years of growing up. She is obsessed with 'good breeding' and fits in well with the neighbours, but not with the children because she demands a different standard of behaviour from that they are used to. Atticus is torn between being courteous to his sister and raising Scout and Jem as he sees fit. After one attempt to try and impose his sister's standards on the children he gives up.

Chapter 14   It requires some adjustment to have Aunt Alexandra living with them. Scout gets into trouble for answering out of turn and Atticus has to refuse his sister's request to get rid of Calpurnia. Atticus has a high regard for their cook, and his sister's arrival does not change that situation. Scout dislikes Jem's new maturity and when he tries to talk to her as though he were an adult she fights him with her fists. Sent to bed as a punishment, Scout is amazed to find Dill hiding under her bed. Atticus is very understanding and, after informing Aunt Rachel, allows Dill to stay the night. Dill tells Scout that he is unwanted at home. Scout cannot conceive of anybody being in that situation because she is so sure of the affection of her father, her brother and Calpurnia.

Chapter 15   Dill is allowed to stay. The peace of summer is broken by troubled events, the significance of which are often lost on Scout. Firstly Heck Tate, the sheriff, and some of Atticus's friends arrive to advise him to give up the case of Tom Robinson; they are worried about the possibility of Tom being lynched. Atticus refuses. A lynch mob from Sarum, bent on killing Tom, arrives at the jail which Atticus is guarding. Jem is worried about Atticus's safety but, unwittingly, it is Scout who diffuses the explosive situation by chatting innocently to Mr Cunningham, who is one of the men. The men in the lynch mob see sense and leave.

Chapter 16   It is not until they reach home that Scout understands the full danger and potential violence of the evening. Atticus tries to explain how people change when in a mob so that normally friendly men, like Mr Cunningham, can become a threat. The next day brings out all the people of Maycomb county, acting as if they were going to a carnival rather than to see a man on trial for his life. Disobeying their father, the children go to the courtroom and find seats amongst the Negroes on the balcony, next to the Reverend Sykes. There they can witness the proceedings without being seen by their father.

Chapter 17   Mr Tate testifies that on being summoned by Mr Ewell he found Mayella with injuries mainly to the right side of her face. Mr Tate also verifies that no doctor had been called. Mr Ewell testifies next. He stirs up the court by his crude language and accusation. He shows his ignorance and stupidity and does not understand the implication of revealing that he is left-handed. Jem understands that a left-handed person would be more likely to have caused the injuries to the right side of Mayella's face. Tom Robinson, being crippled in the left arm, would have found it extremely difficult to inflict Mayella's injuries.

Chapter 18   Mayella Ewell testifies. A picture emerges of her impoverished life, where the relief money is spent on drink, and where she and the children have to cut up old tyres for shoes in winter. Her dreadful loneliness leads us to feel sympathy for her. Although she does not admit it in so many words, it becomes clear that her father probably ill-treats her. The weakness of the accusation that Tom Robinson assaulted her is exposed when he stands up to reveal a withered left arm. Mayella is angry with Atticus because she feels that he has humiliated her in front of everyone and suggested that she is a liar. Mayella says that after doing a job for her Tom Robinson followed her into the house and raped her. By the way Mayella answers Atticus's questions, it appears likely that she is lying. B.B. Underwood spots the children in the court room.

Chapter 19   Tom Robinson testifies; he often did jobs for Mayella and on this particular occasion she asked him into the house and then made advances to him. When Bob Ewell saw Mayella through the window, Tom became frightened and ran away. Scout believes Tom's version of the story. The deep prejudice of the South is very apparent here, especially when Tom admits to feeling sorry for Mayella. The 'impertinence' of his words stuns Mr Gilmer, for no white, however poor, wants or feels they deserve the pity of a Negro. Dill is very upset by this attitude and Scout takes him out of the court, where they meet Dolphus Raymond.

Chapter 20   Outside the court Dill and Scout talk to Mr Raymond. He reveals to them the secret of his drinking bag and explains that because he breaks all the rules of accepted white behaviour it is easier for him and for other people if he pretends to be a social oddity. His faith is in children who have not yet had their innocence tarnished by prejudice. He is glad that Dill has the sensitivity to understand 'the hell white people give coloured folks'. Atticus, in summing up, explains why Mayella might have framed Tom Robinson. He pleads with the jury to weigh the evidence without prejudice; and reminds them that in law all men are equal.

Chapter 21   Calpurnia arrives to say that the children are missing. The children's presence in the court is noticed and they are sent home. Atticus relents and allows them back after their supper to hear the verdict. Jem is optimistic and after a long time the jury return with the result. Tom Robinson is found guilty.

Chapter 22   Jem is outraged with the verdict and Atticus does not attempt to shield him from his new-found awareness of the injustice of Maycomb people. The next day the Negroes send gifts to show their appreciation of Atticus and he is visibly moved. The majority of the neighbours accept the verdict without surprise and feel Atticus was foolish to defend Tom. It is left to Miss Maudie to show the children that there is a glimer of hope because Atticus did affect a small change in the jury's behaviour. He made them think longer. Dill is utterly disillusioned with people and he resolves to separate himself from them when he is older. Bob Ewell insults Atticus by spitting in his face, and threatens future trouble.

Chapter 23   Predictably, Atticus reacts calmly to Bob Ewell's assault, and dismisses the children's fears for his safety by making them look at the situation from Bob Ewell's point of view. Scout and Jem are still worried. Aunt Alexandra feels Atticus is too optimistic about Mr Ewell. Atticus explains to Jem that there can be no fairer system of justice until people's basic prejudices are changed and that will not happen quickly. Atticus reveals that it was a Cunningham who caused the jury to take longer in making up its mind. Initially the Cunningham wanted Tom to be acquitted. Aunt Alexandra dismisses the Cunningham family as being inferior 'trash'. This makes Scout angry as she, unlike her Aunt, does not judge people by their social position. Scout also disagrees with Jem who has worked out there are four kinds of people. To Scout people are just people.

Chapter 24   Aunt Alexandra holds a missionary tea and the ladies of Maycomb attend. They reveal their hypocrisy as they talk with great sympathy about the poor Africans but with no sympathy at all for the local Negroes. Mrs Merriweather talks about the poverty of the Mrunas and about how she cannot understand the 'sulkiness of the darkies'; she also cannot understand why Atticus should want to defend one. Scout is puzzled and unimpressed by the insinuations of the ladies and their leading questions which make her the butt of their amusement. She comments that she prefers the openness of men to these ladies. However, her opinion changes when she sees how Aunt Alexandra conquers her emotions on hearing of Tom's death and manages to continue normally in company. Atticus relates the events surrounding Tom's death in a matter-of-fact way which conveys little emotion; our only clue to his feelings are held in his comment that Tom had 17 bullet holes in him and that 'they didn't have to shoot him that much'. Scout sees her Aunt in a new light, and recognizes that there is more to being a lady than she first imagined.

Chapter 25   Jem and Dill go with Atticus to break the news of Tom's death to his wife, Helen. Dill likens her reaction to being trod on by a giant. This echoes the scene at the beginning of the chapter where Jem admonishes Scout for treading on an insect. The death of Tom is accepted in Maycomb without any surprise and the people remain unmoved by a highly critical editorial in the local paper, where B.B. Underwood is bitter about the needless killing of Tom. Scout finally awakens to the prejudice of Maycomb people and realizes that Tom's case was lost 'the moment Mayella screamed'.

Chapter 26 Scout is growing up. She no longer fears the Radley Place and realizes what a nuisance they must have been to Boo Radley. She is puzzled too by the attitude of her teacher, Miss Gates, who on the one hand condemns Hitler's persecution of Jews but on the other hand sees nothing wrong in their own treatment of Negroes. Miss Gates feels that Tom's conviction will teach the blacks a lesson. Jem does not want to be reminded of the trial as he has not yet come to terms with his disillusionment about people.

Chapter 27 Things begin to settle down after the trial and only three things of interest happen. Bob Ewell begins and is sacked from a job within a few days. He believes Atticus fixed it in some way. Judge Taylor meets an intruder in his house. Helen Robinson is harassed on the way to work by Bob Ewell, until Link Deas makes him stop. Aunt Alexandra senses that Bob Ewell has not yet finally got his revenge and she fears for the safety of their family. Atticus is not so pessimistic. Jem and Scout prepare for the Hallowe'en pageant at school, an event which they have to go to at night, and unescorted.

Chapter 28 The children go to the pageant alone and the darkness and eeriness of the journey across the school yard is stressed. Cecil Jacobs gives them both a fright by jumping out on them. Scout is so humiliated when she misses her cue that she wants to wait until all the audience have left before she and Jem set off home. On the way home they are attacked in the dark by Bob Ewell, who tries to kill them. Jem is badly hurt and Scout is aware of the presence of a fourth person, who saves them and takes the injured Jem home. On their arrival Atticus summons the doctor, who announces that Jem has a broken elbow. Scout is incurious about the stranger on the porch and does not connect him with the fight. The sheriff, Heck Tate, arrives with the news that Bob Ewell has been found dead.

Chapter 29 Scout tells Heck Tate what happened during the attack. Atticus's misjudgment of Bob Ewell is revealed. He did not imagine that Ewell would go to these lengths for revenge. While relating the events it suddenly dawns on Scout that the person who was present at the fight and who saved them was Boo Radley.

Chapter 30 Atticus mistakenly believes that Heck Tate is protecting Jem by insisting that Bob Ewell fell on his knife. Instead it is Boo Radley Heck is trying to shield. Heck argues that it would be wrong to subject Mr Radley to publicity and Atticus finally understands the sheriff's reasoning. Scout likens Boo Radley to a mockingbird. We have no actual proof of who did in fact kill Bob Ewell – evidence for it being either Boo or Jem is available for the reader to weigh themselves, and you should carefully read this and the previous chapter before you come to a conclusion.

Chapter 31 At Boo's request, Scout escorts him to see the sleeping Jem and then home. While thinking of Boo she is reminded of their childish selfishness. They had received gifts from him but given nothing in return. In recalling the events of the past two years she is aware of her greater maturity and of how far she has been able to 'stand in other's shoes'.

Coursework and preparing for the examination

If you wish to gain a certificate in English literature then there is no substitute for studying the text/s on which you are to be examined. If you cannot be bothered to do that, then neither this guide nor any other will be of use to you.

Here we give advice on studying the text, writing a good essay, producing coursework, and sitting the examination. However, if you meet problems you should ask your teacher for help.

Studying the text

No, not just read – study. You must read your text at least twice. Do not dismiss it if you find a first reading difficult or uninteresting. Approach the text with an open mind and you will often find a second reading more enjoyable. When you become a more experienced reader enjoyment usually follows from a close study of the text, when you begin to appreciate both what the author is saying and the skill with which it is said.

Having read the text, you must now study it. We restrict our remarks here to novels and plays, though much of what is said can also be applied to poetry.

1 You will know in full detail all the major incidents in your text, **why**, **where** and **when** they happen, **who** is involved, **what** leads up to them and what follows.

2 You must show that you have an **understanding of the story**, the **characters**, and the **main ideas** which the author is exploring.

3 In a play you must know what happens in each act, and more specifically the organization of the scene structure – how one follows from and builds upon another. Dialogue in both plays and novels is crucial. You must have a detailed knowledge of the major dialogues and soliloquies and the part they play in the development of plot, and the development and drawing of character.

4 When you write about a novel you will not normally be expected to quote or to refer to specific lines but references to incidents and characters must be given, and they must be accurate and specific.

5 In writing about a play you will be expected both to paraphrase dialogue and quote specific lines, always provided, of course, that they are actually contributing something to your essay!

To gain full marks in coursework and/or in an examination you will also be expected to show your own reaction to, and appreciation of, the text studied. The teacher or examiner always welcomes those essays which demonstrate the student's own thoughtful response to the text. Indeed, questions often specify such a requirement, so do participate in those classroom discussions, the debates, class dramatizations of all or selected parts of your text, and the many other activities which enable a class to share and grow in their understanding and feeling for literature.

Making notes
A half-hearted reading of your text, or watching the 'film of the book' will not give you the necessary knowledge to meet the above demands.

As you study the text jot down sequences of events; quotations of note; which events precede and follow the part you are studying; the characters involved; what the part being studied contributes to the plot and your understanding of character and ideas.

Write single words, phrases and short sentences which can be quickly reviewed and which will help you to gain a clear picture of the incident being studied. Make your notes neat and orderly, with headings to indicate chapter, scene, page, incident, character, etc, so that you can quickly find the relevant notes or part of the text when revising.

Writing the essay

Good essays are like good books, in miniature; they are thought about, planned, logically structured, paragraphed, have a clearly defined pattern and development of thought, and are presented clearly – and with neat writing! All of this will be to no avail if the tools you use, i.e. words, and the skill with which you put them together to form your sentences and paragraphs are severely limited.

How good is your general and literary vocabulary? Do you understand and can you make appropriate use of such terms as 'soliloquy', 'character', 'plot', 'mood', 'dramatically effective', 'comedy', 'allusion', 'humour', 'imagery', 'irony', 'paradox', 'anti-climax', 'tragedy'? These are all words which examiners have commented on as being misunderstood by students.

Do you understand 'metaphor', 'simile', 'alliteration'? Can you say what their effect is on you, the reader, and how they enable the author to express himself more effectively than by the use of a different literary device? If you cannot, you are employing your time ineffectively by using them.

You are writing an English literature essay and your writing should be literate and appropriate. Slang, colloquialisms and careless use of words are not tolerated in such essays.

Essays for coursework

The exact number of essays you will have to produce and their length will vary; it depends upon the requirements of the examination board whose course you are following, and whether you will be judged solely on coursework or on a mixture of coursework and examination.

As a guide, however your course is structured, you will be required to provide a folder containing at least ten essays, and from that folder approximately five will be selected for moderation purposes. Of those essays, one will normally have been done in class-time under conditions similar to those of an examination. The essays must cover the complete range of course requirements and be the unaided work of the student. One board specifies that these pieces of continuous writing should be a minimum of 400 words long, and another, a minimum of 500 words long. Ensure that you know what is required for your course, and do not aim for the minimum amount – write a full essay then prune it down if necessary.

Do take care over the presentation of your final folder of coursework. There are many devices on the market which will enable you to bind your work neatly, and in such a way that you can easily insert new pieces. Include a 'Contents' page and a front and back cover to keep your work clean. Ring binders are unsuitable items to hand in for **final** assessment purposes as they are much too bulky.

What sort of coursework essays will you be set? All boards lay down criteria similar to the following for the range of student response to literature that the coursework must cover.

Work must demonstrate that the student:

1 shows an understanding not only of surface meaning but also of a deeper awareness of themes and attitudes;

2 recognizes and appreciates ways in which authors use language;

3 recognizes and appreciates ways in which writers achieve their effects, particularly in how the work is structured and in its characterization;

4 can write imaginatively in exploring and developing ideas so as to communicate a sensitive and informed personal response to what is read.

Much of what is said in the section **Writing essays in an examination** (below) is relevant here, but for coursework essays you have the advantage of plenty of time to prepare your work – so take advantage of it.

There is no substitute for arguing, discussing and talking about a question on a particular text or theme. Your teacher should give you plenty of opportunity for this in the classroom. Listening to what others say about a subject often opens up for you new ways to look at and respond to it. The same can be said for reading about a topic. Be careful not to copy down slavishly what others say and write. Jot down notes then go away and think about what you have heard, read and written. Make more notes of your own and then start to clarify your own thoughts, feelings and emotions on the subject about which you are writing. Most students make the mistake of doing their coursework essays in a rush — you have time so use it.

Take a great deal of care in planning your work. From all your notes, write a rough draft and then start the task of really perfecting it.

1 Look at your arrangement of paragraphs, is there a logical development of thought or argument? Do the paragraphs need rearranging in order? Does the first or last sentence of any paragraph need redrafting in order to provide a sensible link with the preceding or next paragraph?

2 Look at the pattern of sentences within each paragraph. Are your thoughts and ideas clearly developed and expressed? Have you used any quotations, paraphrases, or references to incidents to support your opinions and ideas? Are those references relevant and apt, or just 'padding'?

3 Look at the words you have used. Try to avoid repeating words in close proximity one to another. Are the words you have used to comment on the text being studied the most appropriate and effective, or just the first ones you thought of?

4 Check your spelling and punctuation.

5 Now write a final draft, the quality of which should reflect the above considerations.

Writing essays in an examination
Read the question. Identify the key words and phrases. Write them down, and as they are dealt with in your essay plan, tick them off.

Plan your essay. Spend about five minutes jotting down ideas; organize your thoughts and ideas into a logical and developing order – a structure is essential to the production of a good essay. Remember, brief, essential notes only!

Write your essay
How long should it be? There is no magic length. What you must do is answer the question set, fully and sensitively in the time allowed. You will probably have about forty minutes to answer an essay question, and within that time you should produce an essay between roughly 350 and 500 words in length. Very short answers will not do justice to the question, very long answers will probably contain much irrelevant information and waste time that should be spent on the next answer.

How much quotation? Use only that which is apt and contributes to the clarity and quality of your answer. No examiner will be impressed by 'padding'.

What will the examiners be looking for in an essay?
1 An answer to the question set, and not a prepared answer to another, albeit slightly similar question done in class.

2 A well-planned, logically structured and paragraphed essay with a beginning, middle and end.

3 Accurate references to plot, character, theme, as required by the question.

4 Appropriate, brief, and if needed, frequent quotation and references to support and demonstrate the comments that you are making in your essay.

5 Evidence that reading the text has prompted in you a personal response to it, as well as some judgment and appreciation of its literary merit.

How do you prepare to do this?

1 During your course you should write between three to five essays on each text.

2 Make good use of class discussion etc, as mentioned in a previous paragraph on page 73.

3 Try to see a live performance of a play. It may help to see a film of a play or book, though be aware that directors sometimes leave out episodes, change their order, or worse, add episodes that are not in the original – so be very careful. In the end, there is no substitute for **reading and studying** the text!

Try the following exercises without referring to any notes or text.

1 Pick a character from your text.

2 Make a list of his/her qualities – both positive and negative ones, or aspects that you cannot quite define. Jot down single words to describe each quality. If you do not know the word you want, use a thesaurus, but use it in conjunction with a dictionary and make sure you are fully aware of the meaning of each word you use.

3 Write a short sentence which identifies one or more places in the text where you think each quality is demonstrated.

4 Jot down any brief quotation, paraphrase of conversation or outline of an incident which shows that quality.

5 Organize the list. Identify groupings which contrast the positive and negative aspects of character.

6 Write a description of that character which makes full use of the material you have just prepared.

7 What do you think of the character you have just described? How has he/she reacted to and coped with the pressures of the other characters, incidents, and the setting of the story? Has he/she changed in any way? In no more than 100 words, including 'evidence' taken from the text, write a balanced assessment of the character, and draw some conclusions.

You should be able to do the above without notes, and without the text, unless you are to take an examination which allows the use of plain texts. In plain text examinations you are allowed to take in a copy of your text. It must be without notes, either your own or the publisher's. The intention is to enable you to consult a text in the examination so as to confirm memory of detail, thus enabling a candidate to quote and refer more accurately in order to illustrate his/her views that more effectively. Examiners will expect a high standard of accurate reference, quotation and comment in a plain text examination.

Sitting the examination

You will have typically between two and five essays to write and you will have roughly 40 minutes, on average, to write each essay.

On each book you have studied, you should have a choice of doing at least one out of two or three essay titles set.

1 **Before sitting the exam**, make sure you are completely clear in your mind that you know exactly how many questions you must answer, which sections of the paper you must tackle, and how many questions you may, or must, attempt on any one book or in any one section of the paper. If you are not sure, ask your teacher.

2 **Always read the instructions** given at the top of your examination paper. They are

there to help you. Take your time, and try to relax – panicking will not help.

3 Be very clear about timing, and organizing your time

(a) Know how long the examination is.
(b) Know how many questions you must do.
(c) Divide (b) into (a) to work out how long you may spend on each question. (Bear in mind that some questions may attract more marks, and should therefore take proportionately more time.)
(d) Keep an eye on the time, and do not spend more than you have allowed for any one question.
(e) If you have spare time at the end you can come back to a question and do more work on it.
(f) Do not be afraid to jot down notes as an aid to memory, but do cross them out carefully after use – a single line will do!

4 Do not rush the decision as to which question you are going to answer on a particular text.

(a) Study each question carefully.
(b) Be absolutely sure what each one is asking for.
(c) Make your decision as to which you will answer.

5 Having decided which question you will attempt:

(a) jot down the key points of the actual question – use single words or short phrases.
(b) think about how you are going to arrange your answer. Five minutes here, with some notes jotted down will pay dividends later.
(c) write your essay, and keep an eye on the time!

6 Adopt the same approach for all questions. Do write answers for the maximum number of questions you are told to attempt. One left out will lose its proportion of the total marks. Remember also, you will never be awarded extra marks, over and above those already allocated, if you write an extra long essay on a particular question.

7 Do not waste time on the following:

(a) an extra question – you will get no marks for it.
(b) worrying about how much anyone else is writing, they can't help you!
(c) relaxing at the end with time to spare – you do not have any. Work up to the very moment the invigilator tells you to stop writing. Check and recheck your work, including spelling and punctuation. Every single mark you gain helps, and that last mark might tip the balance between success and failure – the line has to be drawn somewhere.

8 Help the examiner

(a) Do not use red or green pen or pencil on your paper. Examiners usually annotate your script in red and green, and if you use the same colours it will cause unnecessary confusion.
(b) Leave some space between each answer or section of an answer. This could also help you if you remember something you wish to add to your answer when you are checking it.
(c) Number your answers as instructed. If it is question 3 you are doing, do not label it 'C'.
(d) Write neatly. It will help you to communicate effectively with the examiner who is trying to read your script.

Glossary of literary terms

Mere knowledge of the words in this list or other specialist words used when studying literature is not sufficient. You must know when to use a particular term, and be able to describe what it contributes to that part of the work which is being discussed.

For example, merely to label something as being a metaphor does not help an examiner or teacher to assess your response to the work being studied. You must go on to analyse what the literary device contributes to the work. Why did the author use a metaphor at all? Why not some other literary device? What extra sense of feeling or meaning does the metaphor convey to the reader? How effective is it in supporting the author's intention? What was the author's intention, as far as you can judge, in using that metaphor?

Whenever you use a particular literary term you must do so with a purpose and that purpose usually involves an explanation and expansion upon its use. Occasionally you will simply use a literary term 'in passing', as, for example, when you refer to the 'narrator' of a story as opposed to the 'author' – they are not always the same! So please be sure that you understand both the meaning and purpose of each literary term you employ.

This list includes only those words which we feel will assist in helping you to understand the major concepts in play and novel construction. It makes no attempt to be comprehensive. These are the concepts which examiners frequently comment upon as being inadequately grasped by many students. Your teacher will no doubt expand upon this list and introduce you to other literary devices and words within the context of the particular work/s you are studying – the most useful place to experience and explore them and their uses.

Plot This is the plan or story of a play or novel. Just as a body has a skeleton to hold it together, so the plot forms the 'bare bones' of the work of literature in play or novel form. It is however, much more than this. It is arranged in time, so one of the things which encourages us to continue reading is to see what happens next. It deals with causality, that is how one event or incident causes another. It has a sequence, so that in general, we move from the beginning through to the end.

Structure The arrangement and interrelationship of parts in a play or novel are obviously bound up with the plot. An examination of how the author has structured his work will lead us to consider the function of, say, the 43 letters which are such an important part of *Pride and Prejudice*. We would consider the arrangement of the time-sequence in *Wuthering Heights* with its 'flashbacks' and their association with the different narrators of the story. In a play we would look at the scene divisions and how different events are placed in a relationship so as to produce a particular effect; where soliloquies occur so as to inform the audience of a character's innermost emotions and feelings. Do be aware that great works of fiction are not just simply thrown together by their authors. We study a work in detail, admiring its parts and the intricacies of its structure. The reason for a work's greatness has to do with the genius of its author and the care of its construction. Ultimately, though, we do well to remember that it is the work as a whole that we have to judge, not just the parts which make up that whole.

Narrator   A narrator tells or relates a story. In *Wuthering Heights* various characters take on the task of narrating the events of the story: Cathy, Heathcliff, etc, as well as being, at other times, central characters taking their part in the story. Sometimes the author will be there, as it were, in person, relating and explaining events. The method adopted in telling the story relates very closely to style and structure.

Style   The manner in which something is expressed or performed, considered as separate from its intrinsic content or meaning. It might well be that a lyrical, almost poetical style will be used, for example concentrating on the beauties and contrasts of the natural world as a foil to the narration of the story and creating emotions in the reader which serve to heighten reactions to the events being played out on the page. It might be that the author uses a terse, almost staccato approach to the conveyance of his story. There is no simple route to grasping the variations of style which are to be found between different authors or indeed within one novel. The surest way to appreciate this difference is to read widely and thoughtfully and to analyse and appreciate the various strategies which an author uses to command our attention.

Character   A person represented in a play or story. However, the word also refers to the combination of traits and qualities distinguishing the individual nature of a person or thing. Thus, a characteristic is one such distinguishing quality: in *Pride and Prejudice*, the pride and prejudices of various characters are central to the novel, and these characteristics which are associated with Mr Darcy, Elizabeth, and Lady Catherine in that novel, enable us to begin assessing how a character is reacting to the surrounding events and people. Equally, the lack of a particular trait or characteristic can also tell us much about a character.

Character development   In *Pride and Prejudice*, the extent to which Darcy's pride, or Elizabeth's prejudice is altered, the recognition by those characters of such change, and the events of the novel which bring about the changes are central to any exploration of how a character develops, for better or worse.

Irony   This is normally taken to be the humorous or mildly sarcastic use of words to imply the opposite of what they say. It also refers to situations and events and thus you will come across references such as prophetic, tragic, and dramatic irony.

Dramatic irony   This occurs when the implications of a situation or speech are understood by the audience but not by all or some of the characters in the play or novel. We also class as ironic words spoken innocently but which a later event proves either to have been mistaken or to have prophesied that event. When we read in the play *Macbeth*:

> *Macbeth*
>   Tonight we hold a solemn supper, sir,
>   And I'll request your presence.
>
> *Banquo*
>   Let your highness
>   Command upon me, to the which my duties
>   Are with a most indissoluble tie
>   Forever knit.

we, as the audience, will shortly have revealed to us the irony of Macbeth's words. He does not expect Banquo to attend the supper as he plans to have Banquo murdered before the supper occurs. However, what Macbeth does not know is the prophetic irony of Banquo's response. His 'duties. . . a most indissoluble tie' will be fulfilled by his appearance at the supper as a ghost – something Macbeth certainly did not forsee or welcome, and which Banquo most certainly did not have in mind!

Tragedy   This is usually applied to a play in which the main character, usually a person of importance and outstanding personal qualities, falls to disaster through the combination of personal failing and circumstances with which he cannot deal. Such tragic happenings may also be central to a novel. In *The Mayor of Casterbridge*, flaws in Henchard's character are partly responsible for his downfall and eventual death.

In Shakespeare's plays, *Macbeth* and *Othello*, the tragic heroes from which the two plays take their names, are both highly respected and honoured men who have proven their outstanding personal qualities. Macbeth, driven on by his ambition and that of his very determined wife, kills his king. It leads to civil war in his country, to his own eventual downfall and death, and to his wife's suicide. Othello, driven to an insane jealousy by the cunning of his lieutenant, Iago, murders his own innocent wife and commits suicide.

Satire   Where topical issues, folly or evil are held up to scorn by means of ridicule and irony – the satire may be subtle or openly abusive.

In *Animal Farm*, George Orwell used the rebellion of the animals against their oppressive owner to satirize the excesses of the Russian revolution at the beginning of the 20th century. It would be a mistake, however, to see the satire as applicable only to that event. There is a much wider application of that satire to political and social happenings both before and since the Russian revolution and in all parts of the world.

Images   An image is a mental representation or picture. One that constantly recurs in *Macbeth* is clothing, sometimes through double meanings of words: 'he seems rapt withal', 'Why do you dress me in borrowed robes?', 'look how our partner's rapt', 'Like our strange garments, cleave not to their mould', 'Whiles I stood rapt in the wonder of it', 'which would be worn now in their newest gloss', 'Was the hope drunk Wherein you dressed yourself?', 'Lest our old robes sit easier than our new.', 'like a giant's robe upon a dwarfish thief'. All these images serve to highlight and comment upon aspects of Macbeth's behaviour and character. In Act 5, Macbeth the loyal soldier who was so honoured by his king at the start of the play, struggles to regain some small shred of his self-respect. Three times he calls to Seyton for his armour, and finally moves toward his destiny with the words 'Blow wind, come wrack, At least we'll die with harness on our back' – his own armour, not the borrowed robes of a king he murdered.

Do remember that knowing a list of images is not sufficient. You must be able to interpret them and comment upon the contribution they make to the story being told.

Theme   A unifying idea, image or motif, repeated or developed throughout a work.

In *Pride and Prejudice*, a major theme is marriage. During the course of the novel we are shown various views of and attitudes towards marriage. We actually witness the relationships of four different couples through their courtship, engagement and eventual marriage. Through those events and the examples presented to us in the novel of other already married couples, the author engages in a thorough exploration of the theme.

This list is necessarily short. There are whole books devoted to the explanation of literary terms. Some concepts, like style, need to be experienced and discussed in a group setting with plenty of examples in front of you. Others, such as dramatic irony, need keen observation from the student and a close knowledge of the text to appreciate their significance and existence. All such specialist terms are well worth knowing. But they should be used only if they enable you to more effectively express your knowledge and appreciation of the work being studied.

Titles in the series

Pride and Prejudice
To Kill A Mockingbird
Romeo and Juliet
The Mayor of Casterbridge
Macbeth
Far From the Madding Crowd
Animal Farm
Lord of the Flies
Great Expectations
Of Mice and Men
A Man for all Seasons
Jane Eyre